Japan Trivia

装幀 ● 菊地信義
装画 ● 野村俊夫

翻訳 ● トム・ガリー
編集協力 ● 清水宏充
　　　　　エリカ・ヤング　((株) オプティマ)

英語で話す「雑学ニッポン」Q&A
Japan Trivia

素朴な疑問探究会［編］

Bilingual Books

目次

CONTENTS

第2章　日本の「食」の雑学

CHAPTER
2

Trivia on **Japanese Food**

第3章　日本人の「しぐさ」の雑学

CHAPTER 3

Trivia on **Japanese Behavior**

第4章　日本「製品」の雑学

CHAPTER 4 Trivia on **Japanese Products**

CHAPTER 5 Trivia on **Japanese Traditions**

CHAPTER 6 Trivia on **Japanese Tastes**

第7章 「日本語」の雑学

CHAPTER 7 Trivia on **Japanese Language**

第8章　日本の「弱点」の雑学

CHAPTER 8 Trivia on **Japan's Downsides**

まえがき

ニッポンの謎が解ければ
知らなかった自分が見えてくる!

日本人が朝起きる。と、同時に "ニッポンの謎" はスタートする。

日本男性の場合、なぜか左足からズボンをはく人が多い。じつは、これは日本人独特のはき方だ。女性の場合、鏡にむかうと、口紅を下唇から塗りはじめる。これも日本人に独特の行動。外国では上唇から塗りはじめる女性が多いのだ。

なぜ、日本人だけがそうするのか。ともに、江戸期以前からの日本の伝統にルーツがあるというから興味深い。

外国人からみれば、日本人はまさに不思議の国の謎の住人。相手の年齢にこだわり、血液型の話が大好きで、会社を出てからも行動をともにする……。すべて、外国人には「アンビリーバブル!」なのだ。

そのうえ、私たち日本人にとっても、日本は謎の国になりつつある。

なぜ正月に餅や数の子を食べ、日の丸には金の玉がついているのか?……いまの私たちには大難題だ。「日本」を知ることは、自分をよく知ることといえる。

日本と日本人の謎解きを楽しみながら、あなたの不思議を解明してください。

素朴な疑問探究会

PREFACE

Solve the Mysteries of Japan
and You'll Solve the Mysteries of Yourself

The mysteries of Japan begin each morning when the Japanese people wake up.

Why do so many Japanese men put their pants on left leg first? It's a distinctively Japanese method. And why do Japanese women, peering at themselves in the mirror, apply lipstick to the lower lip first? That's also uniquely Japanese. In other countries, most women start with the upper lip.

Why do only Japanese people do these things? Such mysteries are fascinating, for the solutions can be found in traditions that date back centuries to the Edo period and earlier.

To foreigners, Japanese people seem to be the enigmatic residents of an incomprehensible country. Japanese insist on knowing the ages of other people, they love talking about blood types, they spend their free time with people they work with. To people from other countries, it's all unbelievable.

But Japan is becoming a mystery even for Japanese.

Modern Japanese people don't know why they eat rice cake and herring roe at New Year's. Or why Japanese flag pole has a golden ball on the top. For Japanese, learning about Japan means learning about oneself.

So have some fun delving into the mysteries of Japan and the Japanese. Maybe you'll solve some mysteries of your own, too.

Simple Question Research Association

第1章 日本という「国」の雑学

Q: 日本の国旗（日章旗）は、なぜ日の丸になったのか？

A: ———— 日の丸というデザイン自体の歴史は古く、平安時代から存在したという。朱印船でも日の丸を船印につかい、戦国時代には、武田信玄や伊達政宗らが日の丸を旗印に用いた。

　　　　日の丸が国旗として正式に制定されたのは明治3年（1870年）のことだが、それ以前、江戸時代の末期に幕府は「日本総船印は日の丸」と定め、その9年後に起きた生麦事件（1862年）が発端となって、日の丸が国際的に国旗として認知されることになった。

　　開国か鎖国維持かで国論を二分する騒ぎがあったなか、鎖国維持を支持する尊皇攘夷派である薩摩藩島津久光の行列が、行く手を騎馬で横切ったイギリス人4人を殺傷した事件、それが生麦事件（事件が発生した場所の地名が生麦だった）である。

CHAPTER 1 *Trivia on* The Country of Japan

Q: Why was the image of a red sun adopted as the Japanese flag?

A: The red disk depicting a sun—the Hinomaru design—has a long history dating back to the Heian period (794–1185). Trading ships licensed by the shogunate used the Hinomaru symbol, and Takeda Shingen, Date Masamune, and other samurai warlords of the Sengoku, or Warring States, period of the fifteenth and sixteenth centuries carried banners marked with the design.

The Hinomaru was officially adopted as Japan's national flag in the third year of the Meiji period (1870). In 1853 the shogunate had designated it as the symbol for Japanese ships, and nine years after that designation, in 1862, the Hinomaru became known internationally as Japan's national flag at the time of the Richardson Affair (Namamugi Jiken in Japanese).

The Richardson Affair occurred when Japan was engulfed in debate about whether to open up to the outside world or remain closed. Four Englishmen were attacked—one was killed, two injured—after they crossed the path of a procession headed by Shimazu Hisamitsu, leader of Satsuma Province (now Kagoshima Prefecture) and a member of

この事件が発端になり、翌年、薩摩藩とイギリスのあいだで戦争が起こるが、このときの薩摩の艦隊の標識が日の丸だった。日の丸の旗を見たイギリス人が、日本の国旗だと思いこみ、これが日の丸の国際デビューになった。

　その後も、幕府の軍艦咸臨丸が日の丸を掲げて太平洋を初めて乗り越えていき、日の丸は世界に知られるところとなる。つまり日の丸は、先に国際的に日本の国旗として認められた後、国内で正式に日本の国旗（日章旗）と制定されたのである。

Q: なぜ、日の丸の旗竿の上には金の玉がついているのか？

A: ──────── 日本の国旗である日の丸は、白地に赤丸という、じつにシンプルなデザイン。そこで、目立つようにしようということなのか、白黒の段だら縞の旗竿のてっぺんに、金の玉をつけるスタイルが、一般的になっている。

　かつて、この"金の玉"をつけることまで、法律で決められていたことをご存じだろうか。昭和6年（1931年）、石原善三郎なる代議士が議会に「大日本帝国国旗法案」を提出し、そのなかで縞の旗竿と金の玉が正式と記していたが、法案のほうは審議未了のまま立ち消えになってしまった。

　したがって、いまに至るまで、縞の旗竿とそ

the pro-emperor, antiforeigner faction that supported Japan's continued seclusion. (The incident occurred in the village of Namamugi near Yokohama, hence the Japanese name.)

The Richardson Affair set off a war between Satsuma and Britain the next year. The Satsuma fleet fought under the Hinomaru. The British who saw the flag thought that it was the national flag of Japan. This marked the international debut of the Hinomaru.

The flag became internationally known later when the shogunate's battleship *Kanrinmaru* crossed the Pacific Ocean bearing the flag for the first time. Thus, it was only after the Hinomaru was recognized internationally as the flag of Japan that it became officially designated as the country's national flag.

Q: Why does the Japanese flagpole have a golden ball on top?

A: The Hinomaru, Japan's national flag, has a simple design consisting of a red disk on a white background. Perhaps it is to draw attention to this plain banner that the Japanese flagpole usually has black and white stripes and is topped with a golden ball.

But did you know that the use of golden balls was once nearly required by law? In 1931, a Diet member named Ishihara Zenzaburō proposed a bill called the Imperial Japan National Flag Act that would have officially specified the striped flagpole and golden ball. The bill was debated but never passed.

Thus, the striped flagpole with the golden ball on top

の先につける金の玉は、正式のものではないが、しかし、祝日ともなると、この様式の国旗が揚げられるのである。

　一般家庭や商店が、祝日や記念日などに日の丸を掲揚するようになったのは、明治の初期のこと。当初は、国旗をどのように揚げるべきか、ほとんどの人が知らず、それぞれ勝手気ままに白地に赤の旗をつくり、それを物干し竿などに掲げていたという。

　そのうち、縞の旗竿に金の玉、それに国旗の3点セットになったものが売りにだされるようになり、これが市民権を得た。

　一説によると、金の玉は、太陽のつかいであったヤタガラスを象徴したもの、旗竿は、神武天皇のもっていた弓の模様からとったものといわれている。日本神話では、神武天皇東征の際、熊野から大和に抜ける山中で、天照大神から道案内として遣わされたヤタガラスが、神武天皇のもつ旗がついた弓の先に止まったことになっている。

　おそらく、この神話からヒントを得て、国旗3点セットを思いつき、"ヒット商品化"した知恵者がいたのだろう。

Q: 日本人の起源は、なぜはっきりわからないのか？

A: ――――日本列島には、昔から"日本人"という人種（大和民族）が存在し、生活してきたわけではない。大陸や南方の島々から、さまざまな時期

has no official status but is still used for raising the flag on holidays.

Homes and shops began to display the Hinomaru on holidays and anniversaries early in the Meiji period. At first, few Japanese knew how national flags should be displayed, so people would make their own flags of red disks on white backgrounds and raise them on clothes poles or however they liked.

Later, flags were sold in sets with striped flagpoles and golden balls, and that three-part combination became widely accepted.

According to one explanation, the golden ball symbolized the sacred bird Yatagarasu, the servant of the sun, and the stripes represented the pattern of the bow used by Jimmu, the first emperor of Japan. In Japanese legend, when Emperor Jimmu was passing through the mountains from Kumano to Yamato, Yatagarasu showed him the way at the behest of the sun god Amaterasu Ōmikami. In the tale, Yatagarasu rode on the end of Jinmu's bow, from which his banner flew.

It is likely that this myth gave some marketing genius the idea of combining the national flag with the striped pole and golden ball. The result was a hit product.

Q: Why are the origins of the Japanese people so obscure?

A: It is now generally believed that the race called the Japanese (or Yamato) people has not lived in the Japanese archipelago since ancient times. Instead, various peoples migrated

に渡ってきたという説が、ほぼ定説になっている。

　遺伝子を調べてみると、変化した遺伝子数を比較することで、どれくらい前に共通の祖先から分かれたかを知ることができるが、それによると、人類共通の祖先は数百万年前のアフリカで生まれ、数百人ほどの小集団から進化してきたことがわかっている。日本人が、大陸や東南アジアなどから渡ってきた人々の混血であることも、この遺伝子レベルの調査でほぼ解明されている。

　となると、大ざっぱにいうと、約10万年前に登場したといわれるモンゴロイド、すなわちアジア人の祖先が、移動を繰り返すうちに混交し、日本に渡ってまた混交し、しだいに現在の日本人となってきたということになる。

　しかし、この日本人の起源に関する研究は、まだわからないことだらけといっていい。多くの研究者が、それぞれの方法で日本人の起源を追い求め、たとえば耳垢が乾いているか湿っているか、顔の特徴や歯の形状、人間とともに移動したであろう犬の分布など、それはそれはさまざまな手をつかって研究が行われているが、どの地域からの流入が多かったなど、細かい点はほとんどわかっていないのだ。

　わからないのは、それだけ多種多様の人種が、この列島に入りこみ、激しく混交した証拠だとも考えられている。

to the islands from the Asian continent and from islands in the south at different times.

By comparing the number of genes that have changed, it is possible to learn how long ago different groups separated from a common ancestor. Genetic studies tell us that the common ancestors of the human race were born in Africa several million years ago and evolved from a small group of a few hundred people. Such gene surveys have also shown, with near certainty, that the inhabitants of Japan are a mixture of peoples from East and Southeast Asia.

The Mongoloid race that emerged about a hundred thousand years ago—the people who became the ancestors of today's Asians—mixed with native people as they moved from place to place. After some crossed over to Japan, they continued to intermingle with the native population and gradually became the Japanese people of today.

Much is still unknown, though, about the origins of the Japanese. Researchers have used many methods to try to determine where the people of Japan came from. They have looked at whether people's ear wax is wet or dry, at facial features, at tooth shapes, and even at the distribution of dogs that probably migrated together with humans. Nevertheless, almost nothing is known about such details as which region originally had the largest number of immigrants.

The fact that so little is known may itself be proof that this archipelago was populated by many different peoples who intermingled actively.

Q: 日本の国技は、なぜ相撲になったのか？

A: ───────世間一般では、日本の国技は相撲ということに
なっている。そこで、その横綱は、強さ、技と
ともに品位も求められることになる。しかし、
どういうわけか、相撲界には、マスコミを喜ば
せるような下世話な話題が少なくなく、どこが
国技、どこが品位なんだと、感じている人も、
けっこう多いのではないだろうか。

　そもそも、相撲が国技であると、国や法律が
定めているわけではない。

　相撲が国技だといわれるようになったのは、
明治42年（1909年）、最初の常設館である
「国技館」が完成して以来のことである。

　そもそも、自分から国技館などと命名するこ
とが、ふつうの感覚ならやや気恥ずかしいこと
なのだが、この開館の挨拶文で、元大関の大戸
平広吉が、「相撲は日本の国技なり」と述べた
ことが、相撲関係者の自尊心をえらくくすぐり、
それが国技館の名前の由来となったのだ。

　ここから、相撲は国技である、という認識が
世間に広まっていった。もとをただせば、相撲
が国技といわれるようになったのは、建物の名
前に由来するものだったのである。

Q: 日本では、なぜ名前に使える漢字が規制されているのか？

A: ───────以前、わが子に「悪魔」君という名前をつけよ
うとして、お役所に拒否された夫婦がいた。そ

Q: Why is sumo the national sport of Japan?

A: Most people regard sumo as the national sport of Japan, so the grand champions of sumo, the *yokozuna*, are supposed to have not only strength and skill but also character. But the world of sumo produces many trashy stories of the type that delight the mass media so that some people wonder how sumo could ever be a national sport or its wrestlers regarded as having "character."

Actually, the government and laws of Japan have never established sumo as the national sport. Sumo only came to be called a national sport after 1909, when the first permanent sumo facility was completed. It was called the Kokugikan—literally, "national sport building."

Most people would be embarrassed to give their building such a grand name. The title was adopted only after the former champion (*ōzeki*) wrestler Ōtohira Kōkichi declared in a statement on the building's opening that "sumo is the national sport of Japan." His words fired up the self-esteem of people involved in sumo.

Ever since, sumo has been widely regarded as the national sport. The origin of that status, though, can be traced to nothing more than the name of a building.

Q: Why are there restrictions on the *kanji*, or Chinese characters, that can be used in personal names in Japan?

A: Once a local government office refused a couple who attempted to name their child Akuma—literally, "devil."

のとき、「そんな不気味な名前をつけたら、子供がかわいそうだ」「役所が個人の名前にまで口出しする権利はない」と、世論は賛否両論、ほぼ2つに分かれた。

　日本の戸籍法第50条によると、「子の名前には、常用平易な文字を用いなければならない」とある。常用平易な文字とは、常用漢字や人名用漢字、あるいはひらがな、カタカナのことで、現行の戸籍法でつかえる漢字は、いまのところ2928字。

　このなかには、「悪」も「魔」もあり、その意味では「悪魔」でも問題ないはずだが、組み合わせによっては、「将来子供が差別を受けると予想されるなど社会通念上、不適当」として、役所は受理できないケースもあるという。「悪魔」君の場合はそれだったのだろう。

　ところで、人名に用いる漢字が規制されるようになったのは、昭和23年からのこと。きっかけは、現代国語を書き表すためとしているが、実は難読、難解な名前が増えたからで、役所の本音をいうと、「事務処理がめんどうになるので、むずかしい名前をつけるのはやめてくれエ」ということだったのかも知れない!?

Q: 日本では、なぜ陪審制が廃止されたのか？

A: ──────陪審制とは、裁判や法律に素人である一般市民が法廷に入り、被告の有罪・無罪を評決する制

Public reaction was nearly evenly divided between those who felt sorry for any child given such an unpleasant name and those who thought that the government office had no right to interfere with an individual's name.

Article 50 of Japan's Census Registration Law states that "the names of children must be written with commonly used and simple characters," that is, either in the *kanji* designated for everyday use and for personal names or in the *hiragana* and *katakana* syllabaries. This means that under the present Census Registration Law there are 2,928 characters available for use in names.

That list includes both the characters for Akuma, so the parents should have had no problem registering that name. But some character combinations may not be acceptable by government offices if "they are inappropriate under normal social conventions, such as if the child could be expected to suffer discrimination in the future" as a result of the name. This policy seems to have been applied to baby Akuma.

The *kanji* used in personal names were first restricted in 1948. The official reason was to have names written in contemporary Japanese, but another likely explanation is that the government bureaucrats just put a stop to the growing use of difficult names because it was too much trouble to process names that were hard for the bureaucrats to read or understand.

Q: Why was the jury system abandoned in Japan?

A: In the jury system, average citizens who are neither experts on trials nor on the law appear in court to decide whether

度のことをいう。権威主義に陥りやすい裁判を、民主的に運営するために考えだされたシステムである。イギリスで生まれたこの制度は、フランスやアメリカでも導入されて、各国に根づいている。

その形態は、国や州によってかなり異なるが、一般的なのは以下のようなもの。

まず、陪審員は裁判所の管轄地域内に住む16歳から65歳までの男女のなかから選ばれる。条件としては、司法職や聖職に就いていないことで、裁判所によってランダムに選ばれたこの陪審員は、出頭要請があれば裁判が開かれるたびに法廷に集まり、議論を尽くして評決を下すことになる。なお、これは市民の義務であるために、みだりに要請を拒否することはできない。

ところで、日本でも、戦前までこの陪審制が存在していた。本家本元のイギリスに遅れること約700年。昭和3年（1928年）に、日本初の陪審裁判が東京で行われたのである。しかし哀しいかな、日本の陪審員は、陪審裁判を舞台に人間の正義を描いた往年の名作映画『十二人の怒れる男』のようにはいかなかった。

日本語が議論に向かない言語であるのか、日本人が論争を好まない民族なのか、ともかく、初めての陪審裁判の第1回公判では、東京市民のなかから選ばれた12人の陪審員が発した唯一の言葉は、「便所にいきたいのですが……」だったといわれる。

結局、日本では陪審制が根づくことなく、裁判の閉鎖性や法曹界の権威主義などが、現在なお批判され続けている。

a defendant is guilty or innocent. It was a system created to allow trials, which can easily become autocratic, to operate more democratically. Since its birth in Britain, the jury system has become well established in France, the United States, and other countries.

Though it varies much depending on the country, state, or province, in general the jury system operates as follows. First, jurors are selected from among men and women aged sixteen to sixty-five who reside within the district of the court. The jurors are chosen randomly from among those who are not engaged in professions such as law or the government. When requested to appear for a trial, they go to the court to listen to the case and issue a verdict. Participation in a jury is an obligation of citizenship and cannot easily be refused.

Japan also had a jury system before World War II. Japan's first jury trial was held in Tokyo in 1928, some seven hundred years after the system was created in England. Unfortunately, Japanese jurors never became like those portrayed in the film classic *Twelve Angry Men*, which depicted the human search for justice in the context of a jury trial.

Maybe the Japanese language is not suited for debate. Perhaps Japanese people do not like arguing. In any case, it is said that the only words uttered by the twelve jurors selected from among the citizens of Tokyo at Japan's first jury trial were "I want to go to the restroom."

The jury system thus never made inroads in Japan. Critics continue to attack the closed nature of Japanese trials and the authoritarianism of the legal system.

Q: 日本の国有地は、そもそもなぜ国有になったのか？

A: ———— バブル経済の絶頂期、土地をめぐるマネーゲームが日本全国で展開された。とくに、東京を中心とした大都会では熾烈を極め、業者は札びらを切って土地を買いあさり、土地を売らない住人に対しては、一部で悪質な脅しが行われたことも、記憶に新しい。

　そして、その結果がバブルの崩壊であり、住専問題であった。生活感漂う町並みは解体され、土地がらみで動いた金の損失補塡を、何の得もしていない国民が負わされることになった。

　それならいっそのこと、土地をすべて国有地として国が管理し、そこで生活する我々は、国から土地を借りるということにしてはどうか———というような考え方もあるが、しかし国有地にしても、昔から国民の共有財産といった印象は薄く、事実上、役人たちの"私有財産"になっているという声もある。

　明治時代、資本主義が導入されたとき、土地も物件の1つとして取引対象とする考え方が一般化した。ところが、先祖代々、共同で山林などの土地を管理しながら、そこの木を伐って生活を維持してきたような山村の場合、土地の所有権があいまいなため、法律によって強制的に国有地にされることになった。

　そうなったとたん、勝手にその土地に入り、

Q: How did the government come to own land in Japan?

A: At the height of Japan's "bubble economy" in the late 1980s, the entire country was engulfed in a real-estate money game. Wheeling and dealing were especially intense in Tokyo and other big cities, where investors threw away fortunes on land. Many people still remember how residents who refused to sell their land would sometimes be cruelly harassed.

That fever ended a few years later with the bursting of the bubble and the collapse of the real-estate credit loan system. Neighborhoods were destroyed, and the people of Japan, most of whom did not benefit at all from the bubble economy, were forced to make up the money lost in land deals.

Since the situation had become so serious, some people advocated making all land government-owned, and having residents rent land from the national government. Others responded that national land in Japan has never been regarded as property to be shared among the citizens but only as the "private asset" of government bureaucrats.

When the capitalist system was introduced to Japan during the Meiji period (1868–1912), the concept of buying and selling land became widely accepted. In mountain villages, though, where people had been managing forests and other land cooperatively and harvesting trees for their livelihood for generations, property rights to land were unclear, so laws were passed to confiscate the land for the government.

Suddenly it became a crime to set foot on the land or

木を伐ることは犯罪行為になった。このときは
さすがに、多くの人々の抵抗にあい、政府は弾
圧はむずかしいとみると、教育によって、庶民
の怒りを抑えつけることにした。

「国の土地は天皇の土地であり、天皇の土地
に入ろうとするのは、聖域を荒らすのと同じで
ある」と庶民に教えこんだのである。

戦後は、さすがに皇民化教育をもちだすわけ
にいかず、道路や空港など、国の大規模事業に
必要な土地に対して「強制収用」の措置を取っ
てきた。もちろんそれが、すべてではないが、
そうやって収用してきた土地もまた現在の国有
地なのだ。

Q: 日本は狭い国なのに、なぜこんなに人口が多いのか?

A: ──────外国に比べると、日本の人口密度は高い。狭い
島国ながら、人口はけっこう多いのだ。

これはいまに始まったことではなく、昔から
日本は人口の多い国だった。これはわが大和撫
子たちが、特別に多産系だからというわけでは
ない。あえてひと言でいえば、日本人は "元気"
なのだ。

日本人は、さまざまな人種の混血であり、比
較的新しく出現した民族だが、激しい混血の結
果、いわゆる雑種強勢が働いていると考えられ
ている。生物学的にみると抵抗力がかなり強く、
それが日本の人口を維持する根本的な理由にな
っているというのだ。

また、北から南まで、縦に細長い日本の国土

to cut down trees without permission. The government met with widespread resistance that was difficult to suppress, so it tried instead to assuage public anger through education.

The people were taught that "the nation's land belongs to the emperor, and trespassing on the emperor's land would be the same as destroying sacred territory."

After World War II it was no longer possible to treat the people as vassals of the emperor, so the land needed for highways, airports, and other large national projects was taken by force. Some of that seized property has now become national land.

Q: Why does Japan have such a large population when its land area is so small?

A: Compared with other countries, Japan has a high population density, meaning that its population is very large for such a small, island nation.

This is nothing new. Japan has had a sizable population for centuries. The reason is not that the women of Japan have more children but rather that Japanese people have been healthier.

As an ethnic group formed relatively recently from the intermingling of many different races, the Japanese people have benefited from heterosis, or the vigor of variety. Their strong resistance to disease is the fundamental biological reason for Japan's continued large population.

Another factor that has strengthened Japanese vitality is

の自然環境も、日本人の生命力を強くする要因だと考えられている。狭い国土でありながら、北国と南国の寒さ、暑さも、湿気も乾燥も体験できるのが日本だ。その結果、さまざまな環境における抵抗力も強まってきた。

そんな理由で、日本人は、昔から貧しい食生活であっても、かなりの人口を維持してきたというわけだ。戦後、日本が世界一の長寿国となったのも、基本的には同じような理由からと考えられている。

ただ問題は、最近の少子化現象が、将来にどんな影響を及ぼすかということ。

この狭い国には、1億2000万人という人口は、必然的に上限ではないかという意見もある。

Q: 日本人は、なぜ宗教心がうすいといわれるのか？

A: ──────外国で、よく「あなたの宗教はなに？」と聞かれる。そんな質問に、日本人は、臆せず「無宗教」と答えてしまい、驚かれることが多い。

日本では、「無宗教」は当たり前でも、信仰心の厚い人の多い外国では、「無宗教」という答えは、まず考えられないのだ。

そのため宗教を聞かれると、外国では「仏教」と答える日本人は多い。そう答えておけば、相手も納得してくれるからだが、すると、日本通の人に「神道ではないのか？」と聞かれて、ハタと答えにつまってしまうことになる。

だから、外国人と接する機会の多いビジネスマンには、こんな答えを用意している人がいる

the country's natural environment and geography. Japan is long and narrow and stretches from north to south, so residents are exposed to both heat and cold, wet weather and dry. Their physical resistance has thus been reinforced in many different environments.

Despite limited food stocks since ancient times, Japan has been able to maintain a large population. The same factors are thought to be the fundamental reason why, after World War II, Japan achieved the highest longevity of any country in the world.

Japan's problem now is the long-term impact of its declining birthrate. Some people believe that even 120 million does not have to be the maximum population for this small country.

Q: Why are Japanese people said to be not very religious?

A: In other countries, people are often asked what their religion is. When Japanese people reply without hesitation that they have no religion, their listeners are often surprised.

Even though a lack of religious feeling may be considered normal in Japan, such a reply is inconceivable in countries where many people have strong faiths.

When Japanese abroad are asked their religion, many therefore say that they are Buddhist. While that answer will usually be accepted at face value, they may find themselves at a loss if the questioner happens to be familiar with Japan and goes on to ask, "Aren't you Shinto?"

One Japanese businessman who often comes into contact with people from other countries prepared the follow-

という。

「日本の神道には、『四海同胞』という考えがあって、人種や宗教に関係なく、世界のいいところを分けへだてなく取り入れてきました。したがって、いろいろな宗教が混じり合っています」

そして、これが同時に、日本人が宗教心がうすいことの説明にもなっている。家には仏壇や神棚があるのに、クリスマスを祝い、その1週間後には、神社やお寺に初詣でにいくが、これは昔からの神道の『四海同胞』の精神が無意識のうちに身についてしまっているからとも考えられる。

Q: 日本は、なぜ多くの宗教を受け入れてきたのか？

A: ―――― いまの日本人は、北方・南方の両ルートから、この列島に入り込んできた人たちが、混血を繰り返してできあがってきたと考えられていることはすでに述べた。

そのため、日本人の宗教観の根底にも、北方系と南方系の考え方が共存しているといわれる。

簡単にいうと、北方系のシャーマニズムは神がかり信仰のようなもの。たとえば、柏手がその代表で、音をたてることで、神と人間の魂を交流させるという意味がある。

一方、南方系のアニミズムの特徴は、多神教的な信仰観にある。万物に神が宿っているという考え方で、これは日本古来の八百万の神々という考え方につながっている。

ing response. "Shinto has a principle called *shikai dōhō*, or 'All men are brothers.' Japan has adopted the best things from around the world without regard to race or religion. That's why many different religions are combined in Japan."

This helps to explain why Japanese people don't seem to be very religious. When people who have Buddhist and Shinto altars in their homes celebrate Christmas in December and a week later pay New Year's visits to shrines and temples, they show their unconscious acceptance of the Shinto *shikai dōhō*.

Q: Why has Japan been receptive to so many religions?

A: As mentioned above, the Japanese race was formed through the long-term intermingling of peoples who had migrated to the Japanese archipelago from the north and south. The roots of Japanese religious views therefore include both northern and southern strains.

In simple terms, the northern religious strain is a shamanistic, spirit-possessed faith. A typical example is the use of hand-clapping during prayer to achieve contact between gods and men.

The southern strain is more animistic and marked by polytheistic faiths. Gods are believed to reside in all things. This strain is related to the ancient Japanese belief in *yao yorozu*—gods without number (literally, "eight million gods").

そういうベースがあるところに、日本人は仏教を受け入れ、日本古来の神道と混淆させてきた。さらに、儒教の考えも、生活場面での思想として受け入れてきた。一神教世界の国々からすると、信じられない現象といえる。

この理由は、「四海同胞」説をはじめさまざまに指摘されるが、いちばん大きな理由は、「八百万の神々」という発想が根底にあったことが挙げられる。なにしろ「八百万」なのだから、外国から新しい神が入ってきても、へっちゃらなのだ。

また、一時期をのぞいて、宗教が国家統治の原理に利用されなかったこともある。そのぶん、宗教に対する政治的弾圧が比較的少なく、どんな宗教も共存することが可能になったのだ。

日本は、昔から政教分離がすすんでいた国なのだ。

Q: 日本には、なぜこんなに年中行事が多いのか？

A: ———— 正月、節分、雛祭、端午の節句——あげればキリがないほど、日本は年中行事の多い国である。

例の歌を思いだしてほしい。「1月は正月だ。酒が飲めるぞ！」というコンパでおなじみの歌である。12月までえんえんと続くが、こういう歌が成立し、替え歌がいくつでもつくれるほどに、日本には年中行事が多い。

一方、世界には、年中行事と呼べるものが、ほとんどない国もある。熱帯の国々だ。

These beliefs allowed Japanese people to accept Buddhism and to combine it with traditional Shintoism. The philosophy of Confucianism was also accepted in daily life. Such combinations would be inconceivable in monotheistic countries.

Japan's easy acceptance of various religions can be explained by *shikai dōhō* and other theories, but the most fundamental factor is said to be *yao yorozu*. Since there are already "eight million gods," nobody worries about adding a few more from other countries.

A further factor is that religion in Japan has never—except for one brief period—been used as a basis for national unification. This means that there has been relatively little political suppression of religion, and all religions have been able to exist in harmony.

Since ancient times, Japan has been a leader in the separation of church and state.

Q: Why does Japan have so many annual festivals?

A: New Year's, Bean-Throwing Night, Dolls' Day, Boys' Day—the list of annual festivals in Japan goes on and on.

A well-known song often performed at student parties begins, "New Year's is in January. That's when we can drink!" and continues through the other eleven months. The fact that this song exists and has many variations shows that Japan has many festivals in a year.

Elsewhere in the world are countries with almost no annual festivals, such as countries in the tropics.

というと、おわかりだと思うが、日本に年中行事が多いのは、気温、天候の変化に敏感になり、季節が変わるたびにそれにまつわる行事が行われてきたというわけだ。

　また日本のような季節による気温変化の激しい国では、季節のうつろいに敏感でないと、作物をつくることもできなかったという実用的な事情が背景にある。

　ただ、その意味では、年中行事の多さは、日本だけでなく、温帯文化圏共通の現象といえる。とくに日本で多くなったのは、外国の年中行事もどんどん取り入れてきたからだ。

　クリスマス、バレンタインデーを取り入れ、ボジョレー・ヌーボーの解禁騒ぎにまで参加し、ハロウィンにまで手をだそうとしている。

　そういう、外国のものを違和感なく取り入れる日本人の特殊性が、さらに年中行事を増やしてきたともいえるのだ。

　これはなにも、明治以降のことをいっているのではない。日本古来のものに見える年中行事も、ほとんどは中国から取り入れてきたものなのだ。

Q: 日本の都道府県で、なぜ北海道だけあんなに広いのか？

A: ──────北海道の面積は広く、その面積はじつに東京都の38倍。日本の全面積の22パーセントを北海道が占めているほどだ。

　しかし、そんなに広くても、北海道は都道府県の1つとして扱われている。考えてみると、

As you may guess, Japan has so many festivities because its people are very sensitive to changes in temperature and weather. Special activities are also held to mark the changes in the seasons.

There's a practical reason for this as well. In a country where the temperature varies widely with the time of year, farmers would be unable to raise crops if they were not keenly aware of the passing seasons.

For that reason, annual festivities are common not only in Japan but in all cultures with temperate climates. Japan has an especially large number because it has adopted so many additional events from other countries.

Not only are Christmas and Valentine's Day celebrated, but even the annual release of Beaujolais Nouveau stirs up a big fuss. Halloween is starting to be observed as well.

The Japanese people's ready acceptance of foreign customs is thus another factor behind the growing number of annual events.

This openness to foreign celebrations began long before the Meiji period. Most of Japan's traditional events were borrowed from China.

Q: Why is Hokkaido so much larger than Japan's other prefectures?

A: Hokkaido is huge. In fact, this northernmost island is 38 times bigger than Tokyo, and it accounts for 22 percent of Japan's total land area.

Despite its size, Hokkaido is treated as just another prefecture. That seems strange, doesn't it? Why is Hokkaido

変な話ではないか。なぜ、北海道だけあんなに広いのか？　過去に分割しようという話はなかったのだろうか？

　あんなに広くては、なにかの用事のとき、道庁に足を運ぶだけでも大変ではないか。

　まず、その疑問に答えると、北海道民は道庁に用事があっても、いちいち札幌まで足を運ばない。北海道庁には14の支庁があり、他県民が県庁にいくような用事は各支庁ですませることができるのだ。しかし、逆にいえば、14県分くらいの広さがあるということになる。

　じつは、北海道も14県とはいかないまでも、かつては3県に分けられていた時代があった。
　北海道開拓の歴史は、明治維新とともにスタートするが、明治2年（1869年）、開拓使が設置され、本格的な開拓がはじまる。明治15年（1882年）この開拓使はすぐに廃止され、いったん札幌、函館、根室の3県に分割されたのだ。
　しかし、行政単位が分かれていると、やはり開拓がすすめにくいということになって、北海道庁を設置し、北海道全体を管轄するようになった。この長官は戦前は国の任命で、北海道知事が選挙で選ばれるようになったのは戦後のことだ。

　というような経緯で、北海道はいまも広いまま。逆に考えると、行政の効率からして、ほかの県が狭すぎるのかもしれない。

so large? Didn't anyone ever talk about splitting it up?

For with such a large area, isn't it difficult for people to travel all the way to the prefectural capital whenever they have official business?

Let's answer the last question first. When residents of Hokkaido have government business, they don't need to go to Sapporo each time. The Hokkaido government has fourteen subprefectural branches where residents can conduct the business that people in other prefectures can only do at their prefectural capitals. In other words, Hokkaido is equivalent to about fourteen prefectures.

In fact, Hokkaido was once divided up, though into three prefectures instead of fourteen.

The colonization of Hokkaido began at the time of the Meiji Restoration. In 1869, the second year of Meiji, a Colonization Office was set up and the full-scale development of Hokkaido begun. When the office was abolished in 1882, Hokkaido was divided into the three prefectures of Sapporo, Hakodate, and Nemuro.

However, the separation of the administrative functions made it difficult to move ahead with the development, so the Hokkaido government was established and given jurisdiction over the entire island. Before World War II, the governor of Hokkaido was appointed by the national government. Since the war, the position was been filled by popular election.

The island of Hokkaido is large, of course, so from the point of view of administrative efficiency it may be that the other prefectures are too small.

Q: なぜ、昭和天皇の誕生日は祝日として残されたのか？

A: ───────「国民の祝日に関する法律」という法律をご存

じだろうか。日本の祝日は、国会で審議、可決
されたうえで、この法律によって定められたも
のである。

　さて、「国民の祝日に関する法律」が施行さ
れたのは、昭和23年（1948年）のこと。この
時点での祝日は年間9日（現在は14日）で、
「建国記念日」「敬老の日」「体育の日」「みどり
の日」「海の日」などはなかった。

　法律をつくるにあたって重要とされたのは、
伝統は尊重しつつ、神道的・皇室的なものはな
くすことと、名称を平易にすることである。そ
こで、戦前にあった「神武天皇祭」「大正天皇
祭」など皇室の祭典の日はなくなり、「春季皇
霊祭」は「春分の日」、「明治節（明治天皇誕生
日）」は「文化の日」、「新嘗祭」は「勤労感謝
の日」などに、名称を変えている。

　また、我々は、つい戦前の名残で「祝祭日」
といういい方をするが、現在の法律では、皇室
の祭典の日である祭日は存在せず、「国民の祝
日」と呼ぶのが正式である。

　最近設けられた祝日の1つが、「みどりの
日」。昭和天皇が崩御して、「天皇誕生日」が今
上天皇の誕生日の12月23日になったことで、
それまでの「天皇誕生日」（4月29日）が名称

Q: Why is the birthday of Emperor Showa still celebrated as a national holiday?

A: Are you familiar with the National Holidays Law? It requires that national holidays in Japan be deliberated and approved by the Diet.

That law took effect in 1948. At that time, there were nine national holidays; today there are fourteen. The five holidays adopted since 1948 are National Foundation Day, Respect-for-the-Aged Day, Sports Day, Greenery Day, and Marine Day.

When that law was written, emphasis was placed on respecting traditions while eliminating Shinto and imperial elements. The names of the holidays were supposed to be simple as well. Prewar holidays such as the anniversaries of the deaths of Emperors Jimmu and Taisho were eliminated, and the names of other holidays were changed. The Springtime Worship of the Imperial Ancestors became Vernal Equinox Day, the Anniversary of the Birth of Emperor Meiji became Culture Day, and the Harvest Festival became Labor Thanksgiving Day.

Although people still refer to holidays by the prewar name of *shuku-saijitsu*, which has religious connotations, the official name in the present National Holidays Law is *kokumin no shukujitsu*, or people's holidays, because the *saijitsu* events marked by the imperial household are not recognized under this law.

One recently established holiday is Greenery Day. After Emperor Showa died in 1989, the holiday that had celebrated his birthday on April 29 was moved to December 23, the birthday of the present emperor. Emperor Showa's

を変更した「みどりの日」になった。

　国民の祝日関係を担当する総理府の内政審議室によると「みどりの日」は、かならずしも昭和天皇の誕生日だから残されたというわけではなく、ゴールデンウィークの初日だからなくさないでほしいという世論に配慮し、祝日として残したのだそうな。

Q: 日本の道路はなぜ、こんなに狭いのか？

A: ─────昭和31年（1956年）、日本に高速道路を建設するための調査を行ったとき、アメリカから専門家が招かれた。そのときの調査結果は次のようなものだった。

　「工業国で、これほど完全に道路網を無視してきた国は、日本のほかにはない」

　当時の日本の道路事情は、自動車先進国からきた人の目からみると、お粗末としかいいようがなかったようだ。

　しかし、それ以後の日本は、GNP伸び率をはるかに上回るスピードで自動車台数が増加し、それと並行して、高速道路はかなり整備されてきた。

　しかし、問題は一般道路である。都市部では住宅が密集し、道路は狭いままだ。路上駐車で渋滞が生じ、対向車がくるたびに、互いにクルマを左脇に寄せ、サイドミラーを倒してからハラハラしながらすれ違う、なんていう道も存在する。あまりほかの先進国では見

birthday was kept as a holiday under the new name Greenery Day.

According to the Councillors' Office on Internal Affairs, which handles matters relating to national holidays for the Prime Minister's Office, Greenery Day was not established to make the birthday of Emperor Showa. The day remained a holiday in response to popular opposition to losing the first day of the Golden Week holiday period.

Q: Why are Japanese roads so narrow?

A: In 1956, when surveys were being conducted for the construction of expressways in Japan, experts in the field were invited from the United States. Their survey concluded that Japan was the only industrialized country that had ignored its highway network so completely.

In the eyes of people from the world's leading automotive country, Japanese roads were a shambles.

Since then, however, the number of automobiles in Japan has increased at a much faster pace than the GNP, and an extensive network of highways has been built.

The problem now is with regular streets and roads. In urban areas, housing is dense and streets are still narrow. Cars parked on the street create traffic jams, and in some streets, whenever two cars come upon each other in opposite directions, their drivers must squeeze to the left, fold back their side mirrors, and pass each other nervously.

かけない光景だ。

日本の都市の道路が狭い最大の理由は、欧米と違って、馬車交通の時代がなかったためといわれる。

欧米では、馬車がクルマのように人を運び、現在のバスの役割も果たしていたが、日本の場合は徒歩専門。明治時代に入っても、人力車が走る程度で、広い道は必要なかったのだ。

しかも、文明開化の日本は、財布の底をはたいて鉄道の敷設工事に熱をあげたので、予算はもっぱらそちらへまわり、道路建設はまったくかえりみられなかった。戦後、来日したアメリカ人技師から、「ニホンノドーロハ、サイテー！」とバカにされても仕方のないありさまだったのだ。

そして、金持ちの国になった現在もなお、状況はあまり変わっていない。

Q: 日本ではなぜクルマが左側通行なのか？

A: ─────── ご存じのように、アメリカやヨーロッパのほとんどの国では、クルマは右側を走っている。日本と同じように左側通行をしている国は、イギリスやオーストラリア、インドくらいのものだ。

オーストラリアは、その昔、イギリスの植民地。インドもイギリスの植民地である。したがって両国がイギリスにならって左側通行なのはわかるが、どうして日本までも左側通行なのか？

文明開化のころ、鉄道をはじめとして、わが

This is rarely seen in other developed countries.

The main reason Japan's city streets are so narrow is that, unlike Europe or America, Japan never had a period when horse-drawn carriages were the norm.

In the West, carriages carried people as automobiles do today; there were even horse-drawn buses. In Japan, though, the streets were for walking. Even in the Meiji period, the only vehicles were rickshaws, so there was no need for wide roads.

When Japan began to Westernize, it reached deep into its pockets to develop the railways, for that is where its interest lay. Budgets were focused on rail, with little attention paid to road construction. It's no wonder that the American engineers who came to Japan after the war made fun of the terrible roads.

Japan has now become a rich country, but the road situation has changed little.

Q: Why do cars drive on the left in Japan?

A: As you know, cars drive on the right in the United States and nearly all countries in Europe. Only in a few countries—the United Kingdom, Australia, India—do cars drive on the left as in Japan.

Australia used to be a British colony, as was India, so it's easy to understand why those countries drive on the left: they were imitating Britain. But why does Japan also stick to the left?

When Japan was Westernizing, it used Britain as a

国はさまざまな分野でイギリスをお手本にしてきた。そこでクルマに関してもと思いきや、これは違う。

　左側通行の由来は、明治以前にさかのぼるのだ。クルマのなかった時代だから、道を通行するのは、荷馬車や駕籠、そして人であった。人のなかでもエラそうに肩で風をきって歩いていたのは武士で、武士は決まって道の左側を歩いていた。クルマの教習所で習う用語でいえば、「キープレフト」である。

　武士が左側を歩くのには理由があった。腰にさした刀のせいで、ふつう、刀は左側の腰にさすため、とっさのときにそれを素早く抜くには、道の左側を歩く必要があったのだ。

　そうするうちに、武士とぶつかったりして、彼らの機嫌をそこねるようなことになってはたまらない、というわけで、荷車なども、武士に追随して左側通行をするようになったという。この名残で、明治33年（1900年）、人もクルマもすべて左側通行することが決められた

　クルマだけが左側通行となったのは、昭和25年（1950年）のこと。モータリゼーションの時代がきて、それまで左側を歩いていた歩行者が、右側へとはじきだされたかっこうである。

　それを考えると、クルマ社会で「歩行者優先」などというのはキレイごと。クルマが昔の武士のように「どけどけっ」とエラそうに走りまわっているのは、みんなが知っていることである。

model for its railroads and many other things. You might think that automobile driving was copied as well, but in that case you would be wrong.

The keep-to-the-left tradition in Japan dates back even earlier than the Meiji period. There were no automobiles then, so the roads were used only by horse-drawn carts, palanquins, and pedestrians. The latter group included samurai who strutted along arrogantly, always keeping to the left, just as students at driving schools are taught to do today.

The samurai had a reason for walking on the left. The swords they wore at their waists usually hung to the left, so they had to walk on the left side of the road in order to be able to draw their swords quickly.

To avoid bumping into samurai and making them angry, the carts and other passersby followed the samurai and kept to the left. Following this tradition, it was decided in 1900 that both pedestrians and vehicles should keep to the left.

In 1950, the rule was changed and required only cars to stay on the left. As automobile use began to grow, pedestrians were shifted to the right.

Although lip service is paid to putting pedestrians first, in today's car-obsessed Japan everyone knows that cars, like the samurai of old, barge down the roads and force others to get out of their way.

Q: 日本は、なぜどんどん暑くなっているのか？

A: ──────── お年寄りは、よくこんな言葉を口にする。

「昔の夏は、こんなに暑くなかったものだよ。クーラーなんかなくとも、うちわで何とかなったものじゃ」

このお年寄りの実感は正しい。ときどき冷夏の年があるにしても、平均してみると日本列島は確実に暑くなってきている。

その第一の理由は、地球規模での温暖化現象の影響。温暖化現象の原因になる大気圏内の炭酸ガス濃度は、今日も着実に増え続けているのだ。

その影響で、2030年代には、全地球の気温は、現在より1.5〜3.5度も上昇するとの予測もある。過去100年の気温の上昇が0.3〜0.7度であったことと比べると、現在、地球は猛烈な勢いで暑くなっているといえる。

とくに文明国の多い、北緯40度前後で、この傾向は顕著となっている。なかでも飛びぬけた工業国の日本では、この傾向にさらに拍車がかかっている。

また、日本でも、とくに大都市周辺が年々暑さを増している。クーラー、自動車、自動販売機、工場など、大都市の生活と生産が生みだすさまざまな熱が、大都市周辺の温度を急上昇させているのだ。いわゆる「ヒートアイランド現象」というやつだ。

たとえば、東京の月平均の気温である。平年に比べて1度以上高かった月の発生頻度を調べてみると、プラス1度以上の月が1961〜70年

Q: Why is Japan getting hotter and hotter?

A: Elderly people often say, "Summers didn't use to be this hot. We didn't need air conditioners. We got by with hand-held fans."

That feeling of older people is correct. Although Japan occasionally has a cool summer, on average the Japanese archipelago is definitely becoming warmer.

The primary reason is the greenhouse effect. The concentration of carbon dioxide in the atmosphere—the cause of global warming—continues to climb steadily.

This increase in carbon dioxide is forecast to cause a worldwide temperature jump of 1.5° to 3.5°C by the 2030s. Compared to the increase of only 0.3° to 0.7°C over the past hundred years, the earth is heating up at a fierce pace.

This tendency is especially pronounced around the 40th parallel, where many developed nations are located. In Japan, which is one of the most industrialized countries, this factor is advancing even faster.

Temperatures in Japan are steadily rising especially around large cities. Air conditioners, automobiles, vending machines, factories—the heat produced by consumption and manufacturing in major cities is rapidly making the weather hotter. This is referred to as the "heat island" phenomenon.

Let's look at the average monthly temperatures in Tokyo. Between 1961 and 1970, there were 23 months when the temperature exceeded the average by one degree

には23回、71〜80年は26回しかなかったのに
比べ、81〜90年は38回と急増している。

　こういう状況を、環境学者たちは、熱が出る
ほど心配している。

Q: 日本文化はなぜ "カビの文化" といわれるのか？

A: ─────── カビは、気温20〜35度、湿度70パーセントく
らいで、いちばん活発に活動する。つまり、日
本の気候風土は、カビにとっては楽園のような
世界なのだ。

　さて、日本の文化史は、カビとの "2000年
戦争" だったということもできる。日本文化は、
カビと闘うことで成立し、進歩してきたといえ
るのだ。

　まず、生活の根本である住居。日本家屋は、
いつの時代も通気性を最大の狙いとして設計さ
れてきた。高床式の住居、床下と天井裏のスペ
ースを多くした平安以降の様式。それにつれて
発達した襖と障子も通気性を確保するための工
夫だった。

　食べ物も、たとえば餅は表面を硬くすること
で、カビの侵入を許さないという工夫から生ま
れた保存食。衣服も、和服の襟が開きやすくな
っているのは、通気性を重んじたためだ。

　一方、敵に勝つためには敵を知らなければな
らないが、日本人はカビを知りつくし、カビの
力を最大限に利用してきた。日本酒、味噌、納

or more; between 1971 and 1980, there were 26 such months. Between 1981 and 1990, the number leaped to 38.

This situation has made environmental scientists very hot—with worry.

Q: Why is Japanese culture said to be a "culture of mold"?

A: Mold is most active at temperatures between 20° and 35°C and humidities around 70 percent, so the climate of Japan is a paradise for mold.

The cultural history of Japan might even be called a "two-thousand-year war against mold." Japanese culture started out with fighting mold, and it has progressed to fighting mold.

Let's look first at a fundamental aspect of life: housing. Japanese homes have always been designed primarily for good ventilation. This has been the style since the Heian period (794–1185), when houses were built with raised floors, and more space was allocated below floors and above ceilings. The sliding doors and partitions adopted around the same time were also designed to ensure good ventilation.

Food is another example. The rice cakes called *mochi* were invented as nonperishable food because its hard surfaces keep out mold. Clothing also emphasized breathability, as shown by the unfastened collars of kimono.

You must know an enemy in order to defeat it, and the Japanese have known everything about mold and have utilized its powers to the fullest. The manufacture of saké,

豆や醤油は、カビの仲間である菌類の働きなしでつくることはできないのだ。

さらにいうと、日本の国民病といわれた肺結核も、カビの力で克服された。ペニシリンの原材料は青カビなのだ。これが、日本人の発明でなかったのが、不思議なくらいだ。

Q: 日本の消防署の電話番号はなぜ「119番」なのか？

A: ──────火事とケンカが大好きで、ヤジ馬根性が旺盛なのは、江戸っ子の専売特許というよりも、日本人全体に共通した気質だろう。

大正時代には、こんなことがあった。火事が起きると、それを知らせる電話どころか、「火事はどこだ！」という問い合わせが殺到して、電話局側が困り果ててしまったという。そこで、大正6年（1917年）4月1日、電話局は「出火問い合わせはお断り」とし、「出火通知通話制度」を設けた。

この制度は、電話局に電話で火事を知らせると、ただちに消防局につないでくれるというもの。しかし、当初は有料だったために消防局への連絡が遅れることが多く、2年後にやっと無料化された。

さて、電話の自動交換が生まれたのは、関東大震災の大正12年（1923年）のこと。火災報知専用には「112番」が採用された。これは、火事が一刻を争う重大事であるために、ダイヤル時間の短いものとして採用された番号なのだ

miso, *nattō*, and soy sauce depends on the actions of microorganisms that are similar to mold.

In fact, tuberculosis, which was once called the national disease of Japan, was defeated by the power of the blue mold, which is the source of penicillin. It's almost surprising that such a discovery was not made by a Japanese.

Q: Why is 119 the phone number for the fire department in Japan?

A: An attraction to fires and arguments, and a love of gawking at spectacles are said to be the characteristics of residents of Tokyo, but in fact these proclivities are common to all Japanese people.

In the Taisho period, whenever a fire occurred, the telephone company would be deluged with calls—not to report a fire but to ask where it was. So beginning on April 1, 1917, the phone company officially refused to accept questions about fires and adopted a fire notification system.

Whenever a call came to the phone company to report a fire, it would immediately be routed to the fire department. Since they were toll calls, though, the notifications often reached the fire department too late. Two years later, the calls became toll-free.

Automatic phone exchanges were introduced in 1923, the year of the Great Kanto Earthquake, and 112 was adopted as the number to dial for fires. This number was chosen because it could be dialed quickly, as fires were serious and required immediate response. Surprisingly,

が、意外やかけ間違いが多かった。

　というのも、あわてているときというのは、隣の番号をまわすのが、かえってむずかしいものだからだ。あせって、つい111番とか、113番にかけてしまうのだ。

　そこで、昭和2年（1927年）10月1日、消防署の番号は変更され、「119番」に変わった。

　ダイヤルをまわす距離の短い番号を2つ並べ、ひと呼吸おいてから、「1」から遠く離れた位置にある番号をまわす。こういう狙いで「119番」という番号が決定されたのである。「110番」の場合も同じ理由で決まった。

　もっとも最近では、プッシュ式の電話が主流になっているので、このような配慮も意義が薄れてしまっている。

Q: 日本にはなぜ、こんなにもサクラが多いのか？

A: ──────── ♪サクラ　サクラ　弥生の空は見わたすかぎり〜、と歌われるように、サクラの季節になると、それこそ野にも山にも里にも町にもサクラの花を見ることができる。

　日本にサクラが多いのには、2つ理由がある。
　第1の理由は、日本人がサクラが大好きだということだ。サクラの散りぎわの美しさが、日本人の心をとらえ、日本では文学や絵画など、サクラをテーマにした芸術が多く生まれて、サクラが文化や生活に深く密着してきた。
　また、サクラの咲く時期に、進学や就職など

though, the number was often misdialed.

It turned out that dialing the adjacent number on the telephone was in fact more difficult when the caller was in a hurry. People wound up dialing 111 or 113 by mistake.

So on October 1, 1927, the number of the fire department was changed to 119.

First you would dial two quick numbers, pause an instant, and then dial a number far away from the first numbers. That was why 119 was chosen. The police emergency number, 110, was selected for the same reason.

There is less need to consider such factors now that most people use push-button phones.

Q: Why does Japan have so many cherry trees?

A: *Cherry trees, cherry trees.*
     Blooming bright in April breeze...
     Just as the traditional song says, when the cherry blossom season comes, the flowers can been seen throughout the country's fields and mountains, villages and towns.

There are two reasons Japan has so many cherry trees.

The first is that Japanese people like them. The beauty of falling cherry petals captivates the Japanese soul, giving rise to many works of literature and art about cherry blossoms. The cherry tree is an integral part of life and culture in Japan.

The cherry blossom season coincides with the time stu-

が重なるため、日本人が人生の節目節目でサクラのある風景を共通体験しているのも、サクラに対する思い入れを強くしているといえる。

そして、好きな花だから、当然植える機会も増えていく。小学校に植樹される樹木では、現在もサクラが断然トップ。だから、必然的に日本にサクラが多くなるわけだ。

もう1つ、日本の気候風土がサクラにとって育ちやすい環境であることも、大きな理由だ。

欧米にも自生のサクラは存在するが、ほとんどがサクランボの実のなるセイヨウミザクラで、チェーホフの『桜の園』の舞台も、サクランボの果樹園である。

サクラの野生種は、日本には9種類あり、変種を入れると100種類にもなる。さらに人工的に交配したものを加えると400種類にもなり、面積比でみるサクラの木の多さは、群を抜いて世界一である。

dents are promoted in school and workers take on new jobs. This shared association of cherry blossoms with scenes of life's turning points is another reason for the Japanese people's strong affection for the flowers.

And since the blossoms are loved so much, people naturally like to plant the trees. Cherry trees are far and away the most popular tree planted at elementary schools. It's no wonder there are so many cherry trees in Japan.

Another important reason for the trees' abundance is that they grow easily in Japan's climate.

Indigenous cherry trees also grow in Europe and America, but almost all of them are sweet cherries, which bear fruit. Chekhov's play *The Cherry Orchard* is set near an orchard of such trees.

Nine species of cherry tree grow wild in Japan in a hundred different varieties. The number of varieties reaches four hundred if artificially bred types are included. In terms of land area, Japan has the most cherry trees in the world.

日本の「食」の 雑学

Q: 日本人は、なぜお祝いに赤飯を炊くのか？

A: ──── その昔、日本人の生活は、「ケ」と呼ばれる日
常生活と、「ハレ」と呼ばれる神事とに、はっ
きり区別されていた。

米の栽培が日本に伝わる前、日本人は粟や稗
の粥を食べるのがふつうだった。米をつくるよ
うになってからも、相変わらずそれを粥にして
食べていて、その米の粥は姫飯といい、「ケ」
の食事がこれだった。

そのうち、中国から古代の蒸し器である甑が
伝わると、米をふかして食べるようになる。そ
して、ふかした米飯は強飯と呼ばれた。しかし、
強飯を食べるのは「ハレ」のときにかぎられて
いて、まずは神前に供え、儀式が終わったあと、
みんなで分け合って食べるものであった。

ちなみに、現在、もち米を蒸してつくる御強
と呼ばれるものは、強飯の「いい」を省略して、
敬語の「お」をつけたもの。

さて、いまでもめでたいときに炊くお赤飯だ
が、これは、かつて神前に供えるご飯が赤みが

CHAPTER 2

Trivia on Japanese Food

Q: Why do the Japanese make red rice for celebrations?

A: In ancient times, the lives of the people were sharply divided into two parts: *ke*, or daily life; and *hare*, or sacred events.

Before the introduction of rice cultivation to Japan, people mostly ate millet porridge. Even after they began to grow rice, they continued to eat it as a porridge called *himeī*, which was considered *ke* food.

When the Chinese cooking pot called a *koshiki* was introduced to Japan, people began to eat *kowaī*, or steamed rice. However, eating *kowaī* was limited to *hare* occasions, and the food would first be placed before the household shrine. When the ceremony was over, the people present would divide the food and eat it.

Today, steamed glutinous rice is called *okowa*. This word comes from *kowaī* with the final *ī* removed and the honorific prefix *o* added.

Red rice is still eaten on auspicious occasions. That custom originated in the reddish *kowaī* that used to be offered

かった強飯だったことからもきている。小豆を
米といっしょに炊くのは、赤い色をつけるため
の知恵である。

　ちょっと前までは、炊いた赤飯は、親戚や隣
近所に配るものだったが、これも古代から日本
人に受け継がれてきたもので、「ハレ」の日に
強飯を分け合って食べたことの名残といえる。

Q: 日本人はなぜ、めでたい時に尾頭つきを食べるのか？

A: ──────── 祝いの席などめでたいときに、私たち日本人は、
鯛の尾頭つきを食べる。鯛を食べるのは「めで

たい」の「たい」に通じるからだが、祝いの席
ではただの鯛ではダメだ。刺身や切り身ではダ
メで、ここでは断固尾頭つきでなくてはならな
い。

　なぜ、日本人は祝いの席では、尾頭つきにこ
だわるのだろうか？
　めでたい席に尾頭つきの料理がだされるの
は、形が完全にそろっているということで、完
全、すなわち人生を終わりまで全うすることを
象徴している。だから縁起がいいわけだ。
　また、昔の鳥料理には、よく鶴がつかわれた。
鶴は、亀とともに長生きすることから縁起がいい
とされていたからだが、その場合、焼いた肉に
羽や頭の一部がいっしょに皿に盛られることが
多かった。これも一種の尾頭つきだったといえる。
　神事で魚の尾頭つきがでるのは、仏教では殺
生を禁じていて魚を食べないことから、仏教と

to the gods. Adzuki beans are cooked with the rice because they add a red color.

Until recently, people used to give red rice to relatives and neighbors. This custom had been handed down from ancient times, when people used to share *kowaī* on *hare* days.

Q: Why do the Japanese eat fish with the head and tail attached during celebrations?

A: At celebratory banquets, Japanese people eat *tai*, or sea bream, complete with head and tail. *Tai* is chosen because the fish has the same last syllable as the word *medetai*, which means "auspicious." However, not just any kind of sea bream is acceptable at celebrations, and *sashimi* or slices of sea bream are forbidden. Only the entire fish with the head and tail is allowed.

Why do the Japanese insist on including the head and tail at such banquets?

Serving fish with the head and tail intact at celebrations shows that everything is present, thus symbolizing the completeness of life. It's a sign of good fortune.

In the past, people often cooked cranes for fowl dishes. Like tortoises, cranes were thought to bestow good luck because they live a long time. When the crane was cooked, feathers and head were placed on the plates together with the meat, another example of including the entire thing.

The use of fish with the head and tail intact in Shinto ceremonies is thought to emphasize Shinto's difference

の違いを強調するという意味もあったと考えられている。

尾頭つきの料理をだすときの作法としては、左側を頭に、右を尾にする。これは、字を書くときの筆の運びの順序からきていて、字は左から右へと書くからだ。神社に飾られるしめ縄も、たいていは頭は左側、尾は右側になっている。

Q: 日本人は、なぜ正月に数の子を食べるのか？

A: ──────いまは高価な数の子も、昔は肥料につかうような扱いを受けていた。いまでも外国では捨てるのがふつうで、日本人がカネを払って買っていくのは、どうも理解に苦しむことらしい。

ところで、数の子は、黒豆、田作りなどとともに、正月の祝い肴の1つに数えられる。これらはごちそうだから、正月に食べるわけではない。

考えてみればわかることだが、これらはむしろごちそうとはほど遠いものばかりで、黒豆はただの豆にすぎないし、田作りに用いられるカタクチイワシも、数の子と同様、畑の肥料にされたものだ。これらが正月の祝い膳にのぼるのは、数の子は卵が多いことから子孫繁栄を、黒豆はマメで達者を、五万米の別名のある田作りは豊作を意味する、と考えられていたためだ。

さて、これらの3つの祝い肴は、式三献のときに1献ごとにつまむお通しにつかわれてい

from Buddhism, which prohibited the consumption of fish because all killing was banned.

Etiquette calls for these fish to be presented to eaters with the head to the left and the tail to the right, because written brush strokes flow from left to right. The sacred ropes displayed at Shinto shrines are also usually hung with the "head" end on the left and the "tail" end on the right.

Q: Why do the Japanese eat herring roe at New Year's?

A: The eggs of the herring, now expensive, were once so common that they were used as fertilizer. In countries other than Japan, herring roe is still usually thrown away. It must be hard for people in those countries to understand why Japanese pay money for them.

Like black beans and dried anchovies, herring roe is considered one of the celebratory foods of New Year's. But these foods are eaten in January not because they are special treats.

In fact, it doesn't take much thinking to realize that all these foods are far from treats. Black beans are merely beans, and anchovies were once, like herring roe, used as fertilizer. It's thought that these foods are used in New Year's dishes because the large number of herring roe symbolizes fecundity, black beans represent vigor, and dried anchovies—one name for them, *gomame*, can be written with characters meaning "fifty thousand rice"—are associated with bountiful harvests.

These three celebratory foods were eaten one at a time as appetizers in the formal drinking ceremony called *shiki-*

た。式三献とは、大中小の順に3つの盃を台に重ね、上の小盃から順に大盃まで3まわり全員が回し飲みをする儀式のことで、酒がひと回りするごとに食べる肴が祝い肴である。

　よく、宴会の席に遅れると、「駆けつけ3杯！」といって立て続けに3杯、酒を飲まされることがある。これは式三献の名残で、「ほかの者はすでに3回りしてきた盃で酒を3杯飲んだんだから、お前も同じだけさっさと飲め！」ということだ。

　時間をかけてちびりちびりやるのが嫌いな人は、わざと遅れて宴席に着き「駆けつけ3杯、いただきます！」と、自分から声をだして、豪快にグビグビやるといい。これは、礼儀にかなったことなのだ。

Q: 日本人は、なぜ正月にモチを食べるのか？

A: ──── 日本では、正月になるとモチを食べるという風習がある。一説によれば、モチ米が日本に伝えられたのは縄文時代の晩期で、そのモチ米からつくる強飯が神事に供えられていたということから考えると、当時からモチは、ハレの日（特別な行事などのある日）に食べるものとして存在していた可能性があるという。

　しかし、はっきりとモチのことが文献に登場するのは、8世紀ごろのこと。『豊後国風土記』

sankon. In this ceremony, three wine cups of different sizes are placed one on top of the other on a stand, with the smallest cup on top. All participants then drink from the smallest cup first, followed by the medium-sized and the largest cup, going through the entire cycle three times. Every time the wine comes around, each person eats some of the celebratory appetizers.

If someone arrives at the banquet late, the others often shout, "Three cups for coming late!" and make the late-comer drink three cups of saké in a row. This is a hold-over from the *shikisankon* ceremony. The implication is, "Since everyone else has already drunk three cups as they were passed around, you have to drink the same amount right now!"

If you're the kind of person who doesn't like sipping drinks slowly, you can arrive late on purpose, declare, "Three cups for coming late!" and guzzle down the wine quickly. In that case it would be considered good manners.

Q: Why do the Japanese eat rice cakes at New Year's?

A: It is a custom in Japan to eat rice cakes, or *mochi*, at New Year's. According to one explanation, the glutinous rice used to make *mochi* was first brought to Japan in the late Jōmon period (10,000 B.C.–300 B.C.). The steamed rice would be offered to the gods, so from this early period *mochi* may have been eaten on *hare* days when special ceremonies were held.

However, the first written mentions of *mochi* date from much later, around the eighth century. They appear in the

と『山城国風土記』が最初で、いずれも、ある
長者がモチを的にして矢を射ると、モチは白い
鳥になって飛び去ったという話である。

その後、平安時代の『源氏物語』のなかで、
正月に鏡モチを食べる話が初めて出てくる。

鏡モチは、丸い形の鏡をかたどっていること
からこう呼ばれている。その鏡といえば、古来
より日本では神聖なもの。神社のご神体に鏡が
多いのもそのせいで、モチも鏡になぞらえた神
聖なものとして神様に捧げられていたと想像さ
れている。

正月にモチを食べるというのは、神様にお供
えしたもののお下がりをいただき、それによっ
て神様から霊力を授かるという意味合いがあっ
た。これが、日本人が正月にモチを食べるよう
になった理由である。

Q: 日本人は、なぜラーメンを食べるようになったのか？

A: ————戦前、大都会では、夜になると屋台を引いてう
どんやそばを売り歩く商売があった。「夜泣き
そば」「夜泣きうどん」と呼ばれていたものだ
が、これらに混じってチャルメラの音に乗って
売られていた中華そばがラーメンの原型であ
る。しかし、いまのラーメンのようにポピュラ
ーな食べ物ではなかった。日本の食文化にラー
メンが定着したのは、終戦後のことなのだ。

本場中国のラーメンを日本にもちこんだの

historical records *Bungo no kuni fudoki* and *Yamashiro no kuni fudoki*. Both relate that when a certain clan chief shot an arrow at a piece of *mochi*, it turned into a white bird and flew away.

The first recorded instance of *kagami mochi* being eaten at New Year's is found in *The Tale of Genji* from the Heian period. The name *kagami mochi* literally means "mirror *mochi*," after its round shape resembling that of a hand mirror. In ancient times, mirrors were regarded as sacred in Japan, and it is likely—because so often the objects of worship in Shinto shrines were mirrors—that the *mochi* shaped like mirrors would be offered to the gods.

The *mochi* eaten at New Year's was thus leftover religious offerings. It was thought that *mochi* would bring some of the spiritual power of the gods to the eaters. That is why the Japanese acquired the custom of eating rice cakes at New Year's.

Q: Why did the Japanese eat *ramen* noodles?

A: Before World War II, vendors of *udon* and *soba* noodles used to sell their wares on carts that they pulled through the streets of big cities at night. These *yonaki*—literally, "crying at night"—noodle sellers were joined by people who sold Chinese-style *soba* while tooting on double-reed flutes. The Chinese noodles were the precursor of *ramen* in Japan, though they were not as popular then as they are now. It was only after the war that *ramen* became an established part of the Japanese diet.

Genuine Chinese *ramen* was brought to Japan by sol-

は、中国大陸からの帰還兵たちだった。就職も
ままならなかった彼らは、大陸で見覚えたラー
メンのつくり方を思いだし、細々と商売をはじ
めたのである。

　当然、素人の彼らがつくるものは自己流で、
スープの取り方や味付けの仕方、具の種類など、
その人それぞれの流儀でつくられた。そのなか
から、多様なラーメンが生まれてきたわけだ。
味噌や醤油など、日本の調味料による味付けは、
中華そばをアレンジした日本独自の味だ。

　さて、そのラーメンが日本人に人気を呼んだ
のは、安くてそこそこにうまく、そばやうどん
よりも腹持ちがして、貧しい庶民には手ごろな
食べ物だったからだろう。

　こうしてラーメン人口が増えたことで、イン
スタントラーメンというアイデアがわが国で生
まれた。いまや、そのインスタントラーメンは
世界規模のヒット商品になっている。日本流の
ラーメンは、敗戦の思わぬ副産物なのだ。

Q: 日本人が世界一のエビ好きといわれるのはなぜか？

A: ──────歴史をふり返ると、世界でいちばん繁栄してい
る国が、もっともエビを食べているという。そ
こで、現在、世界でもっともエビを食べている
のが日本人。1年で、1人当たり約100匹を食
べているとの調査がある。

　もともと日本人にとってエビは縁起物。長い
触覚と曲がった腰が、ヒゲが長く腰の曲がった
老人に似ていて、長寿を連想させたからである。

diers returning from China after the war. Unable to find work, they remembered recipes for *ramen* that they had learned in China and started their own tiny restaurants.

These amateur cooks had their own individual ways of preparing the noodles; each used different broths, flavorings, and garnishings. This led to a vast number of different styles of *ramen*. The use of *miso* and soy sauce and other Japanese flavorings turned the Chinese noodles into something uniquely Japanese.

Ramen became popular in Japan because it was cheap, tasty, and more filling than *udon* or *soba*. It offered good value for the poor people of that time.

As the number of *ramen* consumers increased, the idea of instant *ramen* was born in Japan. Now instant *ramen* is popular throughout the world.

Japanese *ramen* is thus an unexpected by-product of the country's wartime defeat.

Q: Why are the Japanese called the biggest shrimp-lovers in the world?

A: Throughout history, the richest countries have always been those that consumed the most shrimp, prawns, and lobsters. Now the most voracious crustacean consumers are the Japanese. According to one survey, the average Japanese eats about a hundred of these creatures per year.

Shrimp and their cousins have always been considered an auspicious food in Japan. They suggest long life because, with their long feelers and angular bodies, they

しかし、宴会用の高級食材だったエビが一般家庭でも食べられるようになったのは、小型エビをつかった冷凍エビがきっかけだった。エビは、昭和36年（1961年）に、それまで制限されていた輸入量が、自由化された。そして、その翌年には、ソ連の小型エビをつかった冷凍エビフライが、売りだされている。

　これが、庶民にはショックだったのだ。その当時、エビフライといえば、名古屋ばかりか全国的に高級品である。デパートの食堂や、町の洋食屋さんでしか食べられない。それが、家庭でも食べられるようになったのかと、冷凍エビフライは急速に広まっていった。

　とりわけ弁当のおかずに利用されたことで、需要は高まっていく。エビの輸入量が増えるにつれて、中華、洋食、エスニックと、いろいろな料理につかうようになっていったのである。

　もっとも、歴史をふり返ると、オランダ、イギリスなどかつてエビの消費量がいちばんだった国は、その後、斜陽の道をたどっている。日本も、同じ道を歩もうとしているのだろうか？

Q: なぜ、日本人は変なマナーで洋食を食べるのか？

A: ──────日本人には、洋食を食べるとき、ライスをフォークの背にのせて食べる人がときどきいる。だが、欧米人でそのような食べ方をしている人を見かけることはない。世界中でも、フォークの背にライスをのせ、わざわざ食べにくくして口

resemble bearded, bent-over old men.

This high-class banquet food was eaten in normal households only after frozen shrimp became widely available with the deregulation of imports in 1961. The next year saw the Japanese debut of frozen deep-fried shrimp made from imports from the Soviet Union.

The common people were stunned. At that time, deep-fried shrimp was a luxury both in Nagoya, its traditional home, and throughout Japan. It was available only at department store cafeterias and Western restaurants. As soon as people found out that they could eat it at home, frozen deep-fried shrimp quickly became widely popular.

Demand for shrimp increased, especially as a main ingredient in box lunches. With the increase of imports, shrimp also came to be used in Chinese, Western, and ethnic cooking.

Once the Netherlands and Britain were the biggest consumers of shrimp, but they later lost their place in the rankings. Will Japan's shrimp consumption follow the same path?

Q: Why do the Japanese use the fork differently when eating Western food?

A: When eating Western food, some Japanese people eat rice by placing it on the back of the fork, a practice that is never seen among Americans or some Europeans. Probably the only people in the world who would intentionally eat rice in this difficult way are the Japanese and the English.

に運んでいるのは日本人とイギリス人くらいのものだろう。

じつをいうと、この変なフォークのつかい方は、明治の初期、日本で考えだされたものだ。洋食が日本に入ってきたばかりのころ、ナイフもフォークもさわったことのなかった日本人は、右手にナイフ、左手にフォーク、それぞれ背を上にしてもつようにと教えられた。

すると、根がマジメな日本人、もう最後までそのままの形で食事をするものと思いこんでしまったのだ。だから、付け合わせのライスを食べるときも、フォークをひっくり返すことができず、背にのせるしかなかったのだ。

そのときの間違った思いこみが、洋食を食べるときの日本流のテーブルマナーとして定着してしまったのだという。

また、スパゲティを食べるときにスプーンに麺をのせて、右手にもったフォークでくるくると巻き取るというのも、本場イタリアの正式マナーにはない方法だ。

その昔、イタリア南部では、そうやって食べる人が見られたらしいが、その食べ方が移民によってアメリカにもたらされ、アメリカ人がスプーンをつかうのを見て、日本人もマネするようになったといわれる。

Q: 日本では、なぜ「ダシ」が発達したのか？

A: ──────── 日本人の食事が欧米化してから久しい。牛乳を飲むのも当たり前のことだし、食卓に肉がのぼ

This strange way of using forks was created in Japan in the early Meiji period. Western food had just been introduced to the country, and Japanese people who had never touched a knife or fork before were taught to hold the knife in the right hand and the fork in the left, with the back of each facing upward.

The stubborn, serious Japanese then got the idea that they must continue eating in the same way right through to the end of the meal. Even when eating rice with Western food, they were unable to turn the fork over. They had to put the rice on the back of the fork.

That mistake became established in Japan as good table manners for eating Western food.

The common Japanese practice of eating spaghetti by placing the noodles on a spoon and spinning them around with a fork is not proper manners in Italy, either. Years ago, there may have been people who ate that way in southern Italy. When some of them emigrated to the United States, they took the custom with them. The Japanese then acquired the practice by imitating the Americans.

Q: Why is *dashi* soup broth so popular in Japan?

A: Many years have passed since Western food influences were first introduced to the Japanese. The drinking of milk

るのも、むろん当たり前のことになっている。

　しかし、私たちの遠いご先祖様は農耕民族。
長いこと日本人は、副食はもっぱら野菜に頼っ
ていた。魚とて、海辺の町をのぞけば、頻繁に
食べられるようになったのは、鉄道や道路網、
冷凍技術が発達してからのことなのだ。

　日本で、さまざまな「ダシ」が多用され、ダ
シの味が工夫され続けてきた理由は、野菜主流
の食事だったことにある。

　野菜と対極にある肉、すなわち動物性たんぱく
質や脂肪に富んだ食品は、塩で煮るだけ、焼く
だけで、けっこう、うまみが出るものだ。「ダ
シ」で味をつけていく必要は、ほとんどない。

　ところが、野菜ときたら、ただ茹でても、お
いしく食べることはなかなかむずかしい。そこ
で、脂肪もたんぱく質も少ない野菜をうまく食
べようという工夫で、うまみのエキスである
「ダシ」が生まれ、それが発達したのである。

Q: 日本人は、なぜ漬物が好きなのか？

A: ──────── 日本人は、食料を腐らせて保存する才に長けて
いる。たとえば塩辛である。これは生の魚を発
酵させ、腐りすぎて分解するのを防ぐために塩
を加えたもの。味噌や醤油も、穀物を発酵させ
たものだし、納豆は、大豆を発酵させたもの。
米を発酵させたものが、甘酒であり、日本酒だ。

　漬物は、野菜を発酵させたものと考えていい。
ヌカや麹を加えるのは発酵をすすめるためで、

is now regarded as normal in Japan, and so, of course, is the eating of meat.

Our distant ancestors, though, were agricultural people. For a long time the only side dishes they had available were vegetables. Aside from those who lived near the sea, most people were only able to eat fish after the development of railways, roads, and freezing techniques.

The dominant role of vegetables in the diet is the reason why so many different types and flavors of soup broth, or *dashi*, are used in Japan.

Dishes made from meat—that is, food rich in animal proteins and fats—can taste good just by cooking the meat or boiling it with salt. There is almost no need to flavor it with broth.

However, it's hard to make vegetables taste good just by boiling as they contain little fat or protein, so flavorful broths were developed to give vegetables more taste.

Q: Why do the Japanese like pickles?

A: The Japanese are experts at preserving foods by fermenting them. Take salted fish, for example. It's made by fermenting fresh fish and then salting it to keep it from over-spoiling. *Miso* and soy sauce are made from fermented soybeans and wheat, *nattō* from fermented soybeans, and both sweet and regular saké from fermented rice.

Japanese pickles are a kind of fermented vegetable. Bran and malt are added to promote fermentation, and the

発酵によって生まれた酵素は、人間の体内に入ると栄養分になる。つまり、大根のように繊維と水分が主成分の野菜は、漬物にしたほうがかえって栄養化が高まるというわけだ。

ところで、日本人が漬物を漬けるようになったのは、縄文時代のことといわれる。炭水化物を主食にしていた私たちの祖先は、野菜を副食としていたが、しかし野菜の味だけでは何とも寂しい。

そこで、塩を加えて味をつけてみたところ、独特のうまみや香りが食欲をそそった。また、収穫した野菜を保存するのにも、漬物という方法は最適だ。

そんなわけで、漬物は日本人の食事に欠かせないものとなり、工夫が重ねられてぬか漬け、粕漬け、もろみ漬けなど、さまざまな種類の漬物が生まれて現在に至っているというわけだ。

日本人の知恵と工夫によって生まれた漬物を、その日本人自身がまずいと思うわけがない。だから日本人は漬物好きなのだ。

Q: 日本人は、なぜなんでも丼物にしてしまうのか?

A: ———— 江戸時代、「丼」という器が登場したことは、日本人の食生活にとって画期的なことだった。

なにしろ、それまでは皿が主体で、そばはざるでしか食べられなかった。ところが、丼の出現で温かいかけそばが食べられるようになり、以後は、たまごとじそばやてんぷらそば、きつね、たぬきなど、そばをはじめとする麺類の食

enzymes formed in the fermentation process act as nutrients for the body. Pickling vegetables like *daikon* (giant white radishes), which consist mostly of fiber and water, can make them more nutritious.

The Japanese began to make pickles way back in the Jōmon period. People then ate mainly carbohydrates, with vegetables as side dishes, but their meals must have been plain and dull, as the only flavor was provided by the vegetables.

When people tried adding salt for taste, they found that the resultant flavor and aroma stimulated their appetites. Pickling in salt was also an ideal method for preserving newly harvested vegetables.

Thus pickles became an essential part of the Japanese diet, and many types of pickles—bran pickles, pickles made from saké lees, fermented mash pickles—have been created.

As these pickles were developed by the creative skills of the Japanese, it would be strange if they were thought to taste bad. So that's why the Japanese like pickles.

Q: Why are so many different foods served in bowls?

A: The advent of the *donburi*—a large porcelain bowl—during the Edo period marked a revolution in Japanese eating habits.

Until then, most food was eaten on plates, and *soba* noodles were only eaten cold, served on bamboo screens. With the appearance of the *donburi*, though, it became possible to eat hot soba in a broth. Other ways of serving *soba* and other noodles were also developed: thickened with

べ方はぐんと幅が広がっていった。

　そうなると、日本人は丼のなかに大好きなご飯を盛りたくなる。その上にそばのときと同じようにとじたまごをかけたり、てんぷらを置いて天丼にしたり、またうなぎ丼、親子丼、山かけ丼とさまざまなバリエーションを生んだ。

　さらには西洋料理を丼飯にぶちこんだ牛丼やカツ丼、あるいはカレー丼など、丼料理はとどまるところを知らず、その幅をどんどん広げていった。

　それにしても、日本人は丼物が好きだが、これには日本人の独特の味覚が関係している。ご飯におかずの味がしみて、ご飯とおかずの味が混ざるのが丼物のもち味だが、日本人はこういう味が好きなのだ。

　専門的には「口中調味」というが、日本人は口のなかにいろいろなものを同時に入れて、味をブレンドさせながら食べるのが大好きなのだ。丼物は、その「口中調味」の申し子のような料理といえる。

　また、丼物には工夫しだいで独自のメニューが生まれる楽しさもあり、おかずとご飯が1つの器で食べられる便利さもある。これは器を洗う側にとっても、じつにラクチンときている。そんなこんなで、日本人は丼物が大好きなのだ。

Q: 日本人は、なぜ朝から味噌汁を飲むのか？

A: ──────味噌汁のダシを取るにおいで目を覚まし、食卓

beaten egg (*tamago-toji*), on topped with tempura, fried tofu (*kitsune*), or flakes of fried batter (*tanuki*).

Soon the Japanese also began to fill *donburi* with their favorite food—rice—served in the same way as *soba: tamago-toji*, topped with tempura (to make *tendon*), eel (*unadon*), chicken and vegetables (*oyakodon*), or grated yams (*yamakake-don*), or in many other variations.

The spread of *donburi* dishes knows no limits, as seen in the mixture of Western-style food with rice in dishes like *gyūdon* (rice topped with beef), *katsudon* (rice topped with a pork cutlet), and *karēdon* (rice topped with curry).

This love affair with *donburi* dishes is related to the unique tastes of the Japanese people. The flavor of the *donburi* is created by mixing the taste of the topping with that of rice—a combination that the Japanese love.

The Japanese also love putting a variety of foods into their mouths simultaneously in order to blend the tastes, something a specialist might call "intraoral flavoring." Such intraoral flavoring is epitomized in *donburi*.

Donburi dishes are also fun to make because they can be modified to create unique meals. Plus there's the added convenience of combining both rice and main dish in a single bowl, so there's little time wasted in washing dishes. There are many reasons why Japanese love *donburi*.

Q: Why do the Japanese eat *miso* soup for breakfast?

A: Wake up to the smell of *miso* soup. By the time you reach

に着くころには、味噌汁の香りがぷ～んとただ
よっている。コーヒーの香りもけっして悪くな
いのだが、日本の朝の香りといえば、やっぱり
味噌汁になるだろう。

　ところで、日本人が朝、味噌汁を飲むのには、
かなり深い訳がある。

　日本人の主食の米は、穀類のなかでもっとも
カロリーの高い部類に入るが、残念ながら、塩
分とたんぱく質をほとんどふくんでいない。そ
こで、それらを補うための副食品が不可欠であ
る。それが、味噌汁なのだ。

　ご存じのように、味噌は大豆でつくられてい
て、大豆は畑の肉といわれるほど、良質のたん
ぱく質を豊富にふくんでいる。大豆を発酵させ
て酵素をだし、酵素によって栄養分を増幅した
上で、保存するための塩分が加えられた味噌は、
米のご飯に最適なパートナーといえるのだ。

　遠い昔から、日本人が朝、味噌汁を飲むのは、
これで十分な栄養を補給して、日が沈むまで元
気に仕事に精をだすということだったのだ。

Q: 日本人は、なぜこれほど鍋料理が好きなのか？

A: ──────冬に「なにを食べにいこうか」という相談をす
ると、「鍋にしよう」でまとまることが多い。
日本人が鍋料理を食べるのは、あったまるとい
うのがいちばんの理由だろうが、それ以外に、
鍋料理には、人間が料理に求める4つの機能が
備わっているからだろう。

　その4つとは、まず、みんなで楽しみながら

the breakfast table, the aroma fills the air. While there's nothing wrong with the scent of coffee, it is the smell of *miso* that starts the day in Japan.

But there's a more serious reason why Japanese eat *miso* soup in the morning. Rice, the staple of the Japanese diet, has one of the highest calorie counts of any of the grains, but it contains almost no salt or protein. To make up for these deficiencies, another food is needed. That's where *miso* comes in.

Miso is made from soybeans, and soybeans contain so much good-quality protein that they are called "the meat of the fields." *Miso* is made by fermenting soybeans to create enzymes that boost its nutritional content. The salt is added as a preservative. The result is the ideal accompaniment to cooked rice.

For ages the Japanese have been eating *miso* soup in the morning because it provides enough nutrition for them to work hard for the rest of the day.

Q: Why do the Japanese like one-pot meals?

A: In the winter when people are discussing what to eat, they often decide on meat and vegetables cooked on the table in a pot, or *nabe*. The main reason for eating around a *nabe* is to get warm, but one-pot cooking also provides four other benefits from the food.

First of all, it lets people enjoy eating together.

食べることができるところ。

　2つめは、手間がかからないわりには、栄養のバランスがいいところ。

　3つめは、鍋を囲んだ人すべてが、料理に参加できるところ。

　4つめは、煮えかげん、味のつけ具合を自分の好みでかげんできるところ、である。

　つまり、おいしい料理を食べながら、同じ鍋をつつくという仲間意識が確認できる。みんなの気持ちが、同じ鍋に集まっていることが、日本人には心地よく、うれしいのである。

　それを考えれば、最近鍋を食べて盛り上がったあと、カラオケにいくという行動パターンをとるグループが多いのも当然と言えるかもしれない。

Q: 日本人は、なぜ好んですき焼きを食べるのか？

A: ──────── 坂本九が歌った『上を向いて歩こう』の、アメリカのタイトルは『スキヤキ』。この曲がヒットチャートの1位にランクされる大ヒット曲になったため、「スキヤキ」という名前は、スシ、テンプラ、ヤキトリより以前に、外国人によく知られる日本料理の名前になった。

　さて、日本人はすき焼きが大好きだが、このすき焼き、一説に鋤の上で焼くからともいうが、もともとは好きなものを焼く好き焼きではなく、「すき身焼き」のことだった。すき身とは、うすく切った肉のことで、そのすき身を強い火で焼いて食べるのが本来のすき焼きである。

Second, it is an easy way to get good nutritional balance.

Third, it allows everyone sitting around the pot to partake in the cooking.

And fourth, it lets each person adjust the cooking and flavoring to his or her own taste.

In other words, cooking together in a single pot on the table allows people to share companionship while enjoying good food. For the Japanese, having everyone share in the same pot brings nice, happy feelings.

For that reason, it's not surprising that many people these days go straight from lively *nabe* meals to *karaoke* singing.

Q: Why do Japanese people like *sukiyaki*?

A: The late pop singer Sakamoto Kyū sang a song titled *Ue o Muite Arukō*—"Let's Walk While Looking Up"—that became a number-one hit on the American charts under the title "*Sukiyaki*." This shows that the word was known in other countries even before such words as sushi, tempura, or *yakitori*.

The word "*sukiyaki*" might seem to be derived from *suki*, "like," and *yaku*, "to cook," thus meaning "cook what you like." Another meaning of the word is "cooked on a *suki*," for *suki* is also a "spade." Although Japanese do in fact like *sukiyaki*, the word actually comes from *sukimiyaki*, where *sukimi* means "thinly sliced meat." The origin of

そして、すき焼きの醍醐味は、みんながすき
焼き鍋を囲んで箸でつつくことにある。これは、
囲炉裏の発想から生まれたもので、寒い冬に、
ちゃぶ台の真ん中でぐつぐつと煮える鍋は、囲
炉裏の火のようなものだ。

　それで暖をとりながら、座の盛り上がったと
ころで食べはじめる。すると身も心も温まろう
というものだ。だから、すき焼きは囲炉裏文化
の生んだ産物とも言うべきものであり、日本人
が大好きな料理の1つなのだ。

Q: 日本人は、なぜ腐ったような臭いの食べ物が好きなのか？

A: ──────── 食品用語に「不精臭」というのがある。「不精」
な「臭い」と聞いて想像するのは、靴下や足の
裏の臭いか、腋臭。これらはとにかく嫌われる
臭いだが、じつは、日本人は食品に関しては、
これらに類した臭いが好きなのだ。

　納豆、くさやの干物、古味噌漬などの臭いは、
「不精臭」と呼ばれる。けっしていい匂いでは
なく、むしろ不快な臭いなのに、なぜか日本人
は、これらの臭いの食べ物を好んで食べる。も
ちろん、「くさやの干物なんて、ウンチの臭い
がするのに、よくあんなものが食べられるなァ」
と、顔をしかめる人もいるだろう。しかし、そ
んな人も、漬物や納豆は平気で食べていたりす
る。

sukiyaki was the practice of cooking thin slices of meat over a strong flame.

The real attraction of *sukiyaki* is that everyone sits around the pot together, picking up the food with chopsticks. This practice originated from the old custom of sitting around a central hearth, and the bubbling *sukiyaki* pot set in the middle of a low table in the depth of winter fulfills the same role as the old household hearth.

As people soak up the heat of the cooking flame, the party livens up and everyone starts eating. Both the body and the soul are warmed. Thus *sukiyaki* arose from Japan's traditional hearth-centered homes, and that's why it's one of the favorite foods of the Japanese people.

Q: Why do the Japanese like fermented, strong-smelling foods?

A: *Bushōshū* is a technical word used to describe food smells. Translated literally, it means "unkempt smell," and it brings to mind the odors of socks or feet or armpits. While these odors are indeed unpleasant, when it comes to food, the Japanese people enjoy such smells.

Nattō (fermented soybeans), *kusaya* (dried horse mackerel), *furumisozuke* (old *miso* pickles) all have "unkempt smells." Although the odors are anything but good—in fact, they can be downright unpleasant—for some reason the Japanese like to eat such foods. While some people turn up their noses at certain foods ("I don't see how you can eat that *kusaya*. It smells disgusting!"), those same people are likely not to blink an eye at eating pungent pickles or *nattō*.

「不精臭」の正体は、バクテリアによる発酵で生成される酢酸やプロピオン酸、カプロン酸などといった成分である。いわゆる腐った臭いだから、当然嫌われるものなのだが、その臭いに私たち日本人の食欲がそそられるのは、漬物や納豆を食べて生きてきた日本人にしみついた習性によるもので、そのメカニズムは条件反射に近い。

　"パブロフの犬"みたいなもので、あのくさい臭いを嗅ぐと、条件反射的に食欲が刺激されてしまうわけだ。

　また、欧米では、納豆が近くにあるだけで顔をそむけるような外国人たちが、強烈な臭いのするチーズをうまそうに食べていたりする。チーズもまた不精臭のある食品で、これを食べる西欧人も"パブロフの犬"なのだ。

Q: 日本人は、なぜ塩味の調理を好むのか？

A: ──────── 日本料理と西洋料理の決定的な違いは、水にあるといわれる。日本料理の特徴は、水をたっぷりとつかい、素材の味を生かすことにあり、一方の西洋料理は、水よりも、香辛料やソースをつかい、バターや生クリームなどの濃い味付けを工夫してきた。日本料理が水彩画的であるのに対して、西洋料理は油絵的ということもできるだろう。

　さて、日本人と西欧人の体質を比べてみると、日本人のほうが水っぽいといわれる。日本人の食事がデンプン偏重であるため、体内で分解すると

The components of the "unkempt smells" are acetic acid, propionic acid, caproic acid, and other chemicals created by bacterial fermentation. Since they are the smells of rotting, it's no wonder they are disliked. Nevertheless, they whet the appetites of the Japanese, who have long eaten things like pickles and *nattō*. It's a kind of conditioned response. Like the drooling of Pavlov's dogs, the Japanese, when they smell these odors, get hungry.

While some people in Europe or America might turn their heads rather than get close to *nattō*, some of the same people enjoy eating horribly pungent cheeses. Cheese is another food with an "unkempt smell," and Westerners who eat it are also conditioned, like Pavlov's dogs.

Q: Why do the Japanese like salty foods?

A: The fundamental difference between Japanese and Western cooking is said to be the water used in cooking. Japanese food is prepared with large amounts of water and retains the flavor of the basic ingredients, while Western food is prepared less with water than with spices, sauces, butter, fresh cream, and other full-bodied flavorings. Japanese food is like a watercolor painting, while Western food is like an oil painting.

In fact, the bodies of Japanese people are said to have a more watery content than those of Caucasians. Japanese food is heavy in starch, which turns into moisture and this

きに出る水分が筋肉の中に残りやすいからだ。

また、日本人の主食の米にもその原因はある。

米を主食とすると、血液中のカリウム濃度が増えてくるが、それを抑えるため、我々日本人の体はナトリウムを欲することになる。ナトリウム、すなわち塩。日本人が塩味が好きなのはそのためなのだ。

さらに、塩を摂取すると自然に喉がかわいて水分を補給する。ナトリウムと水分とは、ともに体内に入ると蓄積されやすく、これで血液中のカリウムの割合は減ることになるが、日本人の体は水っぽくて塩分の多いものとなる。

人間も自然の産物の1つといえる。水の豊かな場所に生まれて育つ我々日本人が、水っぽい体をしていて塩分が大好きなのも、自然の摂理からいえば、当然のことだろう。

Q: 日本料理は、なぜ盛り付けにこだわるのか？

A: ────── 外国人が日本料理の盛り付けをみると、「わあ、きれい」と驚くことが多い。しかしその1分後には、「なぜ、ここまで料理の盛り付けにこるのか？」という疑問を投げかける。

そんな外国人に「生け花をする心と同じで、絵を描く心とも通じ、料理に図案するのだ」と、偉大な料理研究家でもあった陶芸家の北大路魯山人の言葉を伝えても、ますます混乱するだけである。外国人には、「料理はおいしければ十分じゃないか」と思っている人が多いのだ。

この外国人の感覚でいうと、たしかに、日本

remains in the muscles.

Another reason for the high moisture content of Japanese bodies is due to the staple food of rice. Eating a lot of rice increases the concentration of potassium in the blood. To reduce the amount of potassium, the body tends to crave sodium, and sodium is essentially salt. That's why the Japanese like salty flavors.

And if you take in a lot of salt, you naturally get thirsty and drink more liquids. Both sodium and water collect easily inside the body. While this reduces the proportion of potassium in the blood, it also makes Japanese bodies wet and salty.

Human beings are just a product of nature. For the Japanese, who are born and raised in a country that has plentiful water, it is only natural that they have watery bodies and crave salt.

Q: Why do the Japanese like to arrange their food so neatly?

A: When foreigners see how neatly Japanese food is arranged on a plate, they often express amazement at its beauty. A minute later, though, they are likely to add, "Why do you make such a fuss about how food is arranged?"

You might try telling them what the great food connoisseur and potter Kitaōji Rosanjin said: "We design food in the same spirit that we arrange flowers or paint pictures." But that will confuse things even more, because many foreigners think that food should taste good and that's enough.

From the point of view of those foreigners, Japanese

料理の盛り付けはこりすぎかもしれない。料理の味に腕を振るえば十分なのに、料理人は盛り付けにまで力を入れる。

日本人は、どんな分野でも、その道を極めようとするが、料理人も、料理の道を極めようとする。盛り付けにまで理屈をつけるのは、そのせいともいえる。

だいたい料理のなにから食べようと、食べる人の勝手なのに、盛り付けで食べる順番まで決めていたりする。外国人にいわせると、料理人が張り切りすぎというわけだ。「料理は、目で味わう」という感覚、これを理解し、納得しているのは、日本人くらいだろう。

Q: 日本人は、なぜことあるごとに酒をくみかわすのか？

A: ──────── 一般家庭でも、酒をつくることは、技術的にはそうむずかしいことではない。が、それをすると、密造になってしまう。しかし、そんなやっかいな法律などなかった時代、酒は味噌や漬物などと同様、それぞれの家で独自につくられていた。

といっても、米がどうしてアルコールに変わるのか、その化学的なメカニズムは、当時の人にはわからない。酔っていい気分になるのも、一種の神秘体験と考えられていた。したがって、客人を招き入れたときに酒をふるまうのは、神がかった最高のもてなしということになり、酒を贈ることは魂を贈ることと同じ。つまり心からの贈り物が酒であり、酒は贈答品の基本となった。

cuisine does put too much emphasis on arrangement. Even though chefs need only show off with the taste of their food, they put a lot of effort into its appearance as well.

The Japanese like to push every field of activity as far as it will go, and chefs are no exception. Since they want to create the ultimate dish, they even apply aesthetic principles to how their dishes look.

Normally the choice about what to eat first should be left to the eater, but with neatly arranged Japanese food even the order is fixed. That's why foreigners think chefs are too obsessed with the appearance of their food. Probably the only people who feel, understand, and agree with the notion that one should also taste food with one's eyes are the Japanese.

Q: Why do the Japanese constantly pour drinks for each other?

A: It's not technically difficult to make saké, but manufacturing it on your own would be bootlegging. However, in the days when there weren't such annoying laws, families used to make their own saké just as they made their own *miso* and pickles.

At that time, people didn't understand the chemical mechanism by which rice turned into alcohol. They regarded the good feeling of being drunk as some kind of mystical experience. Treating guests to saké became the inspired ultimate in hospitality. Sending a gift of saké was the same as sending one's soul, making wine a true gift from the heart. In this way saké became the standard present.

日本人が同じ杯の酒をくみかわすのは、1つ
の器で魂を分け合い、血を分けたも同然の関係
になるという意味がある。親分子分の関係で杯
をくみかわしたり、結婚式での三三九度は、魂
を交流させ、精神的な特別の結びつきを確認す
るものだ。

　　時代を経て現代。仕事が終わって会社の同僚
たちと「どう？　一杯やってかない？」と誘い
合って、酒をくみかわすことがある。これを、
集団でしか行動できない日本人の悪しき行動パ
ターンと分析するむきもあるが、酒をくみかわ
すことによって、帰属意識、あるいは仲間意識
が強まるのは、太古からの日本人の習性といえ
そうだ。ほかの国の人には理解できないかもし
れないが——。

Q: 日本人は、なぜ水割りが好きなのか？

A: ————— バーやスナックでお酒を頼むとき、日本人の半
数以上は水割りを頼む。欧米では、ストレート
か、せいぜいオン・ザ・ロック。わざわざ水で
割って飲む人は少ない。日本だけに水割りが広
まったのは、一つには日本の水がおいしいから
だろう。

　　日本には水の名所が多い。わざわざ車で名水
をくみにいく人もいるほどだが、昔から飲み水
にはこだわってきた。おいしい水をウイスキー
に入れるのは、自然の流れとはいえ、その結果、
洋酒を水割りで飲む人が増えたのである。

For the Japanese, sharing wine out of the same cup symbolizes the sharing of a spirit or the sharing of blood. When bosses and employees exchange drinks, or the bride and groom at a wedding ceremony drink three times from each of three cups, they are bringing their souls together and confirming their special, spiritual relations.

Even in modern times, people often invite their colleagues out for a drink after work. The custom then is to pour drinks for each other. There's a tendency for this to be interpreted as another example of the bad behavior of the Japanese, who are unable to do anything except in groups. But strengthening the feeling of belonging and companionship by sharing drinks has been a Japanese custom since ancient times, and it may be difficult for people from other countries to understand this.

Q: Why do the Japanese like whiskey with water?

A: When ordering whiskey at a bar that serves Western drinks, most Japanese ask for it to be mixed with water. In the West, people prefer their drinks straight or, at most, on the rocks. Few go out of their way to add water. One reason that whiskey is so often watered down in Japan is that Japanese water tastes good.

In fact, many places in Japan are famous for water, so much so that people will drive long distances to get it. This fixation on drinking water dates back a long time, and adding good-tasting water to whiskey is just a natural extension of that attitude. That's why more and more people have come to add water to alcoholic drinks.

また、日本人が酒に弱い人種であることも、水割り派の多い原因になっている。ストレートのウイスキーは、日本人にとって強すぎる酒なのだ。

　そこで、日本の洋酒は、日本人の好みに合わせて、水割りにも適したように開発されているという。ストレートで飲むより、水で割ったほうが飲みやすいから、日本人はせっせと水割りをつくるのだという。

　ちなみに、スコッチは水を入れるとまずくなる。オン・ザ・ロックで飲むとおいしいようにつくられている。

Q: 外国へ行くと、なぜ日本茶が飲みたくなるのか？

A: ──────　せっかく海外旅行に出かけたのなら、そのお国の料理を堪能（たんのう）すればいいものを、3〜4日もすると日本食が恋しくなり、日本食レストランについ足を運んでしまうのが、私たち日本人の悲しい性（さが）。

　そういうレストランでは、値段は日本の何倍もするし、味も日本よりは落ちることが多いはずなのに、出てきた熱い日本茶をすすると、「やっぱり、日本人はコレだよなア」と、満足してしまうのである。

　外国へいった日本人が、日本茶を無性に飲みたくなってしまうのは、生理的な理由がある。日本の食品は、昆布のダシ、味噌、醤油をはじめ、日常的につかわれる味付けの基本料理の多くが、グルタミン酸を大量にふくんでいる。

Another reason is that Japanese get drunk easily. For Japanese, straight whiskey is just too strong.

Western drinks developed in Japan are designed to match this preference for watered-down liquor. Since it's easier to drink with water, the Japanese readily dilute their booze.

However, the taste of Scotch whiskey does not improve when water is added. It's made to taste best when taken on the rocks.

Q: Why do Japanese people overseas get cravings for Japanese tea?

A: An unfortunate characteristic of Japanese people is that when we travel overseas we start to miss Japanese food after only three or four days. While we should be enjoying the cuisine of the country we're visiting, we wind up going to a Japanese restaurant instead.

Overseas Japanese restaurants are several times more expensive than in Japan, and the food can be counted on to be worse. When we sip on the hot Japanese tea served there, though, we're satisfied. "This," we say, "is what the Japanese should drink."

Our unrestrained craving for Japanese tea while overseas has a biological cause. Many of the flavorings normally used in Japanese food—soup stock with pieces of kelp, *miso*, soy sauce—contain large amounts of glutamic acid.

最近では、化学調味料としても、グルタミン酸はふんだんに用いられているから、口にするほとんどすべてのものが、グルタミン酸をふくんでいるといってもいいすぎではない。

また、日本茶独特のうまみもグルタミン酸によるものだし、一部のお茶っ葉には、化学調味料が混ぜられているという話さえある。日本人は、知らず知らずのうちにグルタミン酸を大量に摂取して、一種のグルタミン酸中毒状態になっているといえるのだ。

ところが、外国では、日本ほどグルタミン酸がつかわれない。そこで、数日間、外国に滞在しただけでも、日本人は軽いグルタミン酸の禁断症状を起こすことになるのだ。外国にいって日本茶や日本食が欲しくなるのは、まさしくその禁断症状のせいで、外国で日本人がお茶を一口すすると、とりあえず禁断症状がおさまり、気持ちも落ち着いてくる。

ちなみに、コーヒーや紅茶、中国茶などには、グルタミン酸はほとんどふくまれていない。やはり、日本人は日本茶じゃないとダメなのだ。

Q: なぜ、アユは日本の川にだけ、とくに多いのか?

A: ————川魚の代表格といえば、アユ。釣ったばかりのアユを河原で串刺しにして塩をふり、それを焼いて食べる。淡泊な白身の味とハラワタの香ばしさ、まさに川魚の王者である。

幸いなことに、日本では北海道から沖縄まで、

These days, many artificial flavorings are full of glutamic acid as well, so it would be no exaggeration to say that it is contained in nearly everything we eat in Japan.

The unique taste of Japanese tea is also due to glutamic acid, and it's said that some types of tea leaves are spiked with artificial flavorings. Though we may not be aware of it, we consume so much glutamic acid that we're practically glutamic acid addicts.

But glutamic acid is used less outside Japan. A Japanese spending even a few days abroad comes down with a mild case of glutamic acid withdrawal. Our craving for our native tea and food in other countries is a result of that withdrawal. When we take a sip of Japanese tea, the withdrawal symptoms are relaxed and we calm down.

Coffee, black tea, Chinese tea, and other beverages contain almost no glutamic acid. That's why Japanese people must have Japanese tea.

Q: Why are there so many sweetfish in Japanese rivers?

A: Perhaps the most typical fish in Japanese rivers is the sweetfish. Freshly caught sweetfish are often skewered, salted, cooked, and eaten right on the sandy banks of rivers. The light-tasting flesh and the aroma of their entrails make them the favorite Japanese river fish.

Fortunately, sweetfish—called *ayu* in Japanese—are found

アユは広い範囲に分布している。ところが、日本以外の国となると、せいぜい朝鮮半島と中国の一部地域でみられるだけで、しかも日本の川のように数が多いわけではない。

なぜ、アユは日本の川にだけ多いのか？

答えは、日本の川が急流河川であることにある。

アユは、海から川に入ってしばらくすると、石についた珪藻という藻をさかんに食べはじめる。この珪藻のつく石は流れの急な川底にあり、アユの食欲を満たすほどの珪藻が育つには、水温の比較的高い場所でないと、生長が間にあわない。

さらに、アユは川で生まれ、海に下り、数センチに成長したところでふたたび川に戻ってくるが、1年で死んでしまうために、長い川ではとてもじゃないが、一生を全うすることができない。

そこで、川の下流域が短く、海から上がるとすぐに石の多い川底になり、そこそこに水温の高い日本の川が、アユが生きるには最適な環境といえるのだ。

throughout Japan, from Hokkaido to Okinawa. Elsewhere, though, they are found only in a few areas of the Korean Peninsula and in China, and the number of fish there is smaller than in Japanese rivers.

Why are sweetfish so common only in Japan?

The answer is that Japanese rivers are steep and fast.

Soon after a sweetfish enters a river from the sea, it begins eating large amounts of an algae called diatom. Diatoms grow on stones at the bottom of swift-flowing rivers. In order for the diatoms to grow enough to satisfy the hunger of the sweetfish, the water temperature must be fairly high as well.

Sweetfish are spawned in the rivers and later swim down to the ocean. When they have reached several centimeters in length, they return to the rivers. Since they die after only a year, they can't waste their entire lives swimming up and down long rivers.

As Japanese rivers are short and offer warm, stone-filled beds close to the sea, they provide an ideal environment for sweetfish.

第3章 日本人の「しぐさ」の雑学

Q: 日本人は、なぜ「いってらっしゃい」と手を振るのか？

A: ———— 奈良・平安時代の貴婦人の正装に、領巾と呼ばれた薄くて長い布があった。これは、天女の羽衣のように肩から両腕にかけるものだが、もともとは神に奉仕するときにのみ用いられた。

昔の女性は、これを振って神の魂を奮い立たせ、神を呼び寄せようとしたのである。したがって領巾は呪いの道具で、その呪いの儀式は魂振りと呼ばれていた。

神社で柏手を打つのも、鈴を振るのも、神輿を揺さぶるのも、空気をふるわせることによって神霊を鼓舞しようとするもので、いずれも魂振りの行為のバリエーションといえる。

やがて、この魂振りは、神に対してだけではなく、人に対しても行われるようになり、『万葉集』には、恋人にむけて袖を振る歌が数多く残されている。恋心から、相手の魂を引き寄せるまじないが袖を振ることだったのだ。

さて、日本人が「いってらっしゃい」と手を

CHAPTER 3

Trivia on
Japanese Behavior

Q: Is waving good-bye a Japanese custom?

A: During the Nara and Heian periods, women of the nobility wore long thin garments called *hire* on formal occasions. This was draped over their shoulders and arms like the raiment of a heavenly nymph. Originally it was worn only in religious ceremonies.

In ancient times, women would wave the *hire* in order to cheer up the gods and draw them closer. The garment was an aid to incantation, and the ceremonies in which it was worn were called *tamafuri*, literally, "spirit waving."

The practices of clapping at shrines, ringing bells, and shaking portable shrines are all variations on *tamafuri* as they are aimed at exciting the spirits by stirring up the air.

Later, *tamafuri* came to be addressed not only to the gods but to people as well. In the early poetry anthology called the *Man'yōshū*, there are many poems about women waving their long sleeves at their lovers. The sleeve waving was a charm intended to entice the loved one's soul.

The Japanese adopted the custom of waving when see-

振るようになったのは、バイバイという別れの合図というよりも、もともとは魂振りの意味合いがあった。

昔の人は旅立つ人に手や袖を振ることで神霊を招き寄せ、その神霊の加護によって安全に旅ができるよう祈ったのだ。それがいまに残っている「いってらっしゃい」と手を振ることなのだ。

Q: 日本人は、なぜ人の前を通るとき手刀を切るのか？

A: ──────── 日本人は、人前を通るとき手刀を切る。とくに、歩きすすむ前方のスペースが狭いときなど、前にだした手を振りながら歩いていく。

欧米人はそんなとき、ニコッと微笑んでから通っていく。手刀を切るのは日本人特有のしぐさだが、相手にいらざる不安、緊張を与えないための動作なのである。

目の前に見知らぬ人が近づいてくると、ふつうは少し不安な気持ちになる。たとえ、相手が通りすぎるだけでも、とつぜん襲いかかってくるのではないかという潜在的な不安は捨てきれない。

そこで、欧米の人は目をみて微笑む。微笑むことで、敵意がないことを示すのである。ところが、日本では、「失礼します」といって、手刀を切るようになった。右手をみせることで、武器をもっていないことを示しているのだ。

ing someone off not as a casual gesture of good-bye but instead as a kind of *tamafuri*. When seeing off travelers in ancient times, people would wave their arms and sleeves to invite the sacred spirits to provide protection for a safe journey. That custom survives today as the practice of waving at people who are leaving.

Q: Why do the Japanese make a chopping motion with one hand while passing in front of others?

A: When one Japanese person passes in front of another, the first makes a brief chopping motion with the right hand. Called *tegatana*—literally "hand sword"—this gesture is especially common when the space ahead is narrow. People often make their way through cramped areas with one hand chopping up and down.

In a similar situation, Westerners would smile at each other. The *tegatana* is a unique Japanese gesture. Its purpose is to avoid making the other person nervous unnecessarily.

When approached by a stranger, we normally feel a sense of unease. It's hard to get rid of the unconscious fear that a passerby might suddenly attack us.

That's why Westerners smile: a smile shows that you feel no hostility. The Japanese instead adopted the custom of saying "excuse me" and making a chopping motion with the hand. By showing our right hand, we indicate that we are not holding a weapon.

また、手刀を切ることで、自分の通る道を示すという意味もある。それによって相手の領域と自分の領域に一線を画し、「そこから先の、あなたの領域には入らないですよ」という意志を表現しているのである。

　そのとき、腰をかがめて通るのも、控えめで、つつましいのが美徳とされる日本独特の動作である。

Q: 日本では、なぜ握手が広まらないのか？

A: ──────明治以後、日本人は、欧米の習慣をどんどん受け入れてきた。洋服を着て、髪型を洋風に変え、机と椅子で仕事をするのが当たり前になった。

　しかし、あいさつだけは別だ。握手というごく基本的な習慣は、受け入れなかったのだ。いまでも、誰とでも平気で握手するのは、永田町の先生たちくらいだ。

　なぜ、握手はいまだに定着しないか？　ある心理学者によると、日本人の心理には、身体的な接触をともなうあいさつがなじまないのだという。

　身体的な接触は、無防備な自分を見せあうコミュニケーション手段になり、その意味では、握手は、お互いの心をひらくためのなかなかいいあいさつ法といえるという。

　しかし、日本人は、自分の気持ちが相手にストレートに伝わるのが、どこか面映ゆく思ってしまう国民。初対面ではなかなかオープンにな

Another purpose of this gesture is to show the direction you are walking, thus designating the boundary between your territory and the other person's territory. It seems to say, "I will not encroach on your domain."

Bowing slightly at the same time is another uniquely Japanese gesture, for it suggests the modesty and reserve that are prized in Japan.

Q: Why hasn't shaking hands caught on in Japan?

A: Ever since the Meiji period, Japanese people have adopted many customs from the West. Now, as a matter of course, the Japanese wear Western clothes, sport Western hair styles, and work at desks while sitting on chairs.

Greetings, though, are different, and the basic custom of shaking hands has never become popular. About the only people who will shake hands with anyone are politicians.

Why hasn't shaking hands caught on? According to one psychologist, the Japanese psyche cannot adapt itself to a greeting that involves bodily contact.

As a method of communication, body contact shows the participants to be defenseless. In that sense, shaking hands is an excellent way for people to open up to each other.

As a nation, though, the Japanese are shy about expressing their feelings to others directly. It's difficult for them to open up to people they have just met. Only as they get to

れず、つきあううちに徐々に距離を縮めながら、コミュニケーションをすすめていく。

そういう日本人には、距離をとって頭を下げ合う、おじぎのほうがぴったりなのだそうだ。

永田町の先生たちが握手好きなのは、それだけ面の皮が厚いから――といっているのではない。

Q: 日本人は、なぜ電車に乗ると居眠りをするのか？

A: ─────── 日本では、電車のなかで居眠りをしている人が多い。とくに、昼下がりの空いた電車内では、こっくりこっくりしている姿を何人も見かけることがある。

そんな光景に驚くのが来日直後の外国人。電車のなかで、よく眠れるなあと不思議に思うらしい。

たしかに、多くの国では、電車内で寝ていると、スリのかっこうの標的になる。近くに寄ってきて、サイフを抜かれたり、ナイフでバッグを切られて、中身を盗られることがある。それに比べると、日本の昼間の電車は、ゆっくり眠れるぐらい安全だということもある。

しかし、それ以上に指摘される理由は、電車のなかでこそゆっくり休んでおこうという心理が働くからだという。それだけ、日本人は疲れているのだ。

とくに、サラリーマンは、職場や取引先、訪問先で想像以上に緊張している。

そのため、ひと仕事終えて電車に乗るとホッとする。だからつい居眠りしてしまうというのである。

know somebody well do they gradually bridge the gap and engage in real communication.

Instead of shaking hands, Japanese remain at a distance and bow. Bowing seems more suitable for them.

We hope this doesn't suggest that the reason Japanese politicians like to shake hands is that they feel no shame.

Q: Why do the Japanese fall asleep on trains?

A: In Japan, many people sleep on trains. On an uncrowded train in the afternoon you are likely to see several people dozing off.

This surprises foreigners who have just come to Japan. They think it's weird that people can sleep on trains like that.

In many countries, falling asleep on a train will make you a sitting duck for pickpockets. They'll sneak up to you and slip out your wallet or cut the straps of your handbag and steal whatever is inside. In contrast, Japanese trains in the daytime are safe enough to take a nap.

But even more important is the feeling that trains are a place where the Japanese can relax. That shows how tired they are.

White-collar employees in Japan are under incredible stress in their workplaces and wherever they go on business, so when work is finished and they get on a train they just let themselves unwind. That's why so many fall asleep.

スーツ姿のサラリーマンが、電車のなかで居眠りしていたら、ひと仕事終えてホッととひと息ついている証拠。ゆっくり休ませてあげてほしい。

Q: 日本人の"星空"の描き方は、なぜ特殊なのか？

A: ──────── 日本の子供と外国の子供とは、星の描き方がずいぶん違う。日本の子供には、銀色や黄色のクレヨンで、適当に星をちりばめる子が多い。しかも、夜空に均等に描こうとする。

「このへん、星が少ないから、もうちょっと描いておくか」

という雰囲気なのである。そういうと、自分の子供のころもそうだったという方が多いかもしれない。

　ところが、外国の子供は、そんな星の描き方はしない。星を描くときはかならず星座を描くのである。星座がわかるように、星と星を線で結ぶ子供も少なくない。

　これは、子供のころから星座に親しむ機会が多いか少ないかの違いだが、日本人が星座にあまり興味を示さないのは、農耕民族だったからではないかといわれている。

　狩猟民族や遊牧民族など、つねに移動している民族は、星座や北斗七星を目印に、方角を定めた。星座が生活と密着していたのである。

　だから、星にまつわる伝説も多いし、詩もたくさん謳われている。そのため、子供のころか

If you see a salaryman in a suit sleeping on a train, it's proof that he has finished work and is taking a breather. Let him rest.

Q: Why do the Japanese draw the night sky differently from other people?

A: In Japan, children draw stars very differently from other countries. Japanese children use silver and yellow crayons to draw stars, scattering the stars evenly throughout the night sky. They think that if there are fewer stars in one section of the picture, then they should add more there. Many Japanese adults will remember having the same urge when they were children.

Foreign children, though, do not draw stars that way. They always draw stars in constellations. Many children even indicate the constellations by connecting the stars with lines.

This reflects the difference between how children are exposed to learning about constellations. Because Japan used to be an agricultural nation, the Japanese are indifferent to constellations.

Hunting or nomadic peoples who were constantly on the move would use the Big Dipper and other constellations as guides. Constellations were an important part of their lives.

These races had many legends and songs about stars. Even today the children's early contact with stars and with

ら、星や伝説や詩にふれているから、星の描き
方も違ってくるのである。

しかし、農耕民族だった日本では、星で方角
を知る必要がない。それより、農作業の目安に
なる月の満ち欠けには敏感で、月にまつわる昔
話や詩歌も多い。

日本の子供は、満月や三日月など、月の形に
ついては、外国の子供よりうるさい。

Q: 日本のサラリーマンは、なぜ会社を出た後も一緒に行動するのか？

A: ————— どの会社にも、行きつけの飲み屋というのがあ
る。仕事が終わると、仲間うちで、アイコンタ
クトだけで行き先のわかるような飲み屋があ
る。

たしかに日本のサラリーマンは、仕事を終え
会社を出るとその種の飲み屋に集まることが多
い。仕事が終わってもいっしょに行動するわけ
だが、まっすぐ家へ帰るのがふつうの外国人に
は理解に苦しむ行動だという。これは、日本の
サラリーマンに、会社がいちばん大切という人
がいかに多いかの証拠にほかならない。

というと、「オレは、そんなことはない」と
いう人もいるだろう。しかし、頭のなかでは否
定しても、奥さんや子供の病気や出産を理由に
会社を休める人は少ない。また、家族との約束
と仕事のどちらを優先するかと問えば、やはり
仕事と答える人が多いのが、日本の特徴である。

legends and songs about them make them draw stars differently.

However, for the agricultural Japanese there was no reason to learn the location of the stars. More important were the phases of the moon, which were used as guides for farming. There are many myths, poems, and songs about the moon in Japan.

Japanese children are more picky about full moons, crescent moons, and other moon shapes than are children in other countries.

Q: Why do Japanese salarymen hang out together after work?

A: Every company in Japan has its regular watering holes. When the work day is over, coworkers, with just a wink or a glance, can tell each other which bar they will be going to.

Japanese salarymen often gather at such drinking places after work. This practice of staying together after work is hard to understand for people from countries where workers normally go straight home. This is proof that for many Japanese white-collar workers nothing is more important than their company.

Some salarymen will deny this. Despite such denials, though, few men take off work when their wife or children are sick, or even when their wife is giving birth. Japan is unique in that if you asked working men which was more important, family commitments or work, most would answer "work."

これは、欧米人とは違って、個人や家庭より組織を優先するのが日本社会の行動基準だからである。仕事後も、会社の人と行動をともにしないと、仲間はずれになったようで不安になってしまうのである。

　ある心理学者にいわせると、原因は、ズバリ「自分のアイデンティティが弱いから」。アイデンティティ、すなわち自分が自分であることの根拠がしっかりしていれば、たとえ「仲間はずれ」のようなことになっても、弱気になったり、焦ることはなくなる。

　入社直後の調査で、「会社がいちばん大切」と答えるという人は減ったが、彼らも、出世競争が激しくなると、徐々に「会社人間」へと変身していく。

Q: なぜ、日本人はモノを受け取るとき両手をそろえるのか？

A: ──────名刺をもらうときに、両手をそろえる日本人を見て、外国人は、「オイ、オイ、名刺がそんなに重いのか？」と疑問に思うという。

　ところが日本では、新入社員研修で、「名刺は、両手で受け取ること」と教えられる。名刺は、相手の人格を象徴したものだから、両手でおしいただかないと、失礼になると考えられているからである。

　しかし、それが外国人にはわからない。彼らにとって、名刺は名刺以外の何物でもない。初対面のときは、ビジネスがうまくいくためのお

Unlike the West, Japanese society places greater emphasis on the organization than on the individual or the family. Even after work, people worry about being left out if they don't hang around with people from the office.

According to one psychologist, the cause is nothing other than a weak sense of self. If people had a firmer grasp of their personal identities, they would not be timid or nervous about being left out of the group.

Recent surveys show that fewer new employees identify the company as the most important part of their lives. But even such younger workers, as they face tougher competition for promotion, will gradually be transformed into loyal company men.

Q: Why do the Japanese hold out both hands when receiving an object?

A: When a foreigner sees a Japanese holding out both hands to receive someone's business card, he wonders, "Hey, is the card really that heavy?"

New employees in Japan are trained to receive name cards with both hands. Since the cards are a symbol of the person, it is considered impolite if they are not received respectfully with two hands.

But this explanation will not be understood by foreigners. For them, a business card is just a business card. Some foreigners seem to think that this gesture is some kind of

まじないかと思う人もいるという。

　また、日本では卒業証書をもらうときも両手
で受け取る。とくに目上の人に対しては、両手
で受け渡しするのがていねいと考えられている
からである。

　この感覚も外国人にはわからないらしい。外
国人は校長先生などから渡される卒業証書など
も平気で片方の手で受け取ったりしている。

Q: 日本の女性は、なぜ下唇から口紅を塗るのか？

A: ───────電車のなかで、口紅を塗る日本の若い女性に、
アメリカ人が驚いていた。欧米では、人前で化
粧をするのは、その筋の女性というのが常識だ
からだが、そのアメリカ人は、もう1つ驚いて
いたことがある。

　その女性が、下唇から口紅を塗っていたこと
である。アメリカ女性をはじめ、欧米の女性は
上唇から塗るのがふつう。下唇から塗る女性を
めったに見ないからである。

　ところが、日本には下唇から塗る人がだんぜ
ん多い。日本で下唇が先になるのは江戸時代の
化粧法の影響だという。

　江戸時代、多くの女性は、口紅を下唇しか塗
らなかった。歌舞伎をみてもわかるが、女形は
下唇にしか口紅を塗っていないが、それにくわ
えて、明治以降、第2次世界大戦まで、水商売
の女性以外、上唇に塗らなかった。

　そのため、戦後、上唇を塗るようになっても、

magic spell used at first meetings for smooth business relations.

The Japanese also use both hands to receive diplomas. The polite two-handed gesture is considered especially appropriate when receiving something from a superior.

Foreigners, on the other hand, see no problem with receiving a diploma from a principal with only one hand.

Q: Why do Japanese women put lipstick on their lower lip first?

A: An American woman was once surprised to see a young Japanese woman on a train applying lipstick. One reason for her surprise was that, in Europe and America, the women who put on makeup in public are likely to be barmaids, prostitutes, or others of that ilk. But she had another reason to be surprised as well. The Japanese woman was applying lipstick to her lower lip first. In America and Europe, women normally start with the upper lip. Rarely does one see women applying lipstick to the lower lip first.

In Japan, though, the lower-lip-first group is by far the larger. The practice is said to reflect the makeup custom of the Edo period. At that time, most women painted only their lower lips. Even today, Kabuki actors who play female roles apply rouge only to their lower lip, and from the Meiji period through World War II, the only women who applied lipstick to their upper lips as well were women of the night.

When coloring the upper lip became popular after the

下唇から先に塗るのが作法となったのである。そして、その作法が、いまでも受け継がれているというわけだ。

　もっとも、最近のファッション雑誌の記事には、欧米のファッション雑誌のパクリ企画が多い。写真も、口紅を上唇から塗る場面がつかわれていたりして、そんな雑誌を参考にしている若い女性には、上唇から塗る人も増えている。

Q: 日本人は、なぜ大晦日に夜ふかしをするのか？

A: ─────子供には、年に何日か、夜ふかしを許される日がある。大晦日もその1つだが、日本人が大晦日に夜ふかしするのは、テレビで『紅白歌合戦』をみるからではなく、もともと中国の習慣にならったからだという。

　その昔、中国には、元旦の朝まで起きていて、新しい年の初日の出を見守るという習わしがあった。これを「守歳」と呼んだが、この習慣が日本にも伝わり、大晦日は寝ないというのが一般的になった。

　さらに日本で、この習慣は、近くの神社やお寺にこもって元旦を迎えるというふうに変化していった。たとえば、お寺では、除夜の鐘をつき、108の煩悩を打ち払う儀式が行われた。

　やがて、この神社やお寺にこもるという習慣が、家で夜を過ごし、明け方に家から神社やお寺に初詣でにいくようになったのである。その昔、地方には、「大晦日に寝ると白髪になる」

war, doing the bottom lip first was considered correct, and that practice is still followed today.

Many of the articles in Japanese fashion magazines today are direct copies of European or American magazine articles. The photographs often show lipstick being applied to the upper lip first, so that method is being used by more young women who follow the magazines.

Q: Why do the Japanese stay up all night on New Year's Eve?

A: There are few days in the year when Japanese children are allowed to stay up until morning. One of them is New Year's Eve. People stay up all night not because they want to watch the annual televised song competition that airs that evening. Rather they are following a Chinese custom.

It was the tradition in ancient China to stay up until New Year's morning and watch the first sunrise of the year. This is called *shusai* in Japanese—literally, "protect the year." The custom was adopted in Japan, where it became normal practice not to sleep on New Year's Eve.

This practice later included spending the night at a nearby shrine or temple and greeting New Year's Day there. Buddhist temples held a ceremony in which a New Year's bell was rung 108 times to drive away the 108 earthly desires.

Later, instead of spending the night at a shrine or temple, people would stay home at night and pay New Year's visits to those sacred places early the next morning.

In the countryside, people used to say that sleeping on

とか、「シワが増える」という言い伝えもあった。

Q: 日本人は、なぜ温和な性格の民族といわれるのか?

A: ─────── オウム関連のサリン事件や誘拐事件の続発で、日本の評判は悪くなっている。しかし、日本が、世界でももっとも安全な国の1つであることは、間違いない。

世界でも、深夜、女の子が繁華街から自宅まで1人で帰れる国は珍しい。なぜ、日本は治安がいいか? その根本的な理由は、日本人の性格が比較的温和なことにある。

その理由を次のように説明している人がいる。

アジア人のほうが、ヨーロッパ人よりも非戦闘的で、気質が温和なのは、季節が暑熱・寒冷のどちらも激しい変化を示さず、平均しているところに、その主因がある。すなわち、精神の衝撃や体の激しい変調が起こらないため、気質が始終同一の状態に保たれずに猛々しくなったり、無鉄砲や勇猛になったりということが少ないからだ……。

じつは、この分析をしたのは、ギリシアの哲学者・医学者であったヒポクラテス。紀元前400年のことである。それから、約2,400年たっているのだが、この説明は、いまでも当てはまるかもしれない。

日本のなかでも、さらに気候のいい静岡、和歌山、沖縄の人たちの性格は推して知るべしで、自分たちのことを「静岡ボケ」と称したりする。

New Year's Eve would make your hair turn white and your skin wrinkle.

Q: Why do the Japanese have such placid personalities?

A: Although the subway gas attacks by the Aum Shinrikyō cult and some brutal kidnappings have damaged Japan's reputation, there is still no doubt that Japan is one of the safest countries in the world. In few other countries can a young woman return home from an entertainment district late at night all by herself.

Why is Japan so safe? The fundamental reason for this is the relatively placid nature of the Japanese.

One person has explained the reason as follows. Asians are less combative and more peaceful than Europeans mainly because the Asian climate is moderate, without sharp seasonal swings from hot to cold. The absence of such psychological shocks and sudden changes in body condition means that people seldom lose their temper or become brash and impetuous.

This analysis was made by the Greek philosopher and physician Hippocrates, who lived around 400 B.C. Although some 2,400 years have passed since then, his explanation may still apply.

Even within Japan you can guess at the personalities of people who live in places like Wakayama, Okinawa, and Shizuoka, where the climate is especially mild. In Shizuoka,

もちろん、のんびりしていて、争いを好まず、
温和な性格のことである。

Q: 日本人は、なぜ欧米人より体臭が弱いのか？

A: ──────欧米人やアラブ人に比べて、日本人の体臭は弱
いといわれる。それは、日本人に、アポクリン
腺をもっている人が少ないからである。

アポクリン腺とは、わきの下や乳首の周囲、
恥毛部分に分布している汗腺のことをいう。こ
こから出る液自体は無臭だが、肌にすみついて
いる細菌がその分泌液を分解すると、強烈な臭
いになる。

白人や黒人には、このアポクリン腺をもって
いる人が多いのに、日本人の90パーセントは、
退化している。臭いの素そのものが断たれてい
るのである。

もっとも、欧米では、あの臭いがセクシーだ
といって、できるだけ臭いのきつい人を探して
いる人もいるそうだ。

Q: なぜ、日本人の歩き方は、せわしないのか？

A: ──────マラソンのテレビ中継を見ていると、日本人と
外国人とでは、走るときのストライド（歩幅）
がぜんぜん違う。外国人が3歩走るあいだに、
日本人は5歩ぐらい走っている。

じつは、その姿は、ふつうの人の歩く姿と同

for example, people refer to themselves as *Shizuoka boke*, or "Shizuoka space cases." The term refers to relaxed, uncombative people with placid personalities.

Q: Why do Japanese people have less body odor than Westerners?

A: The Japanese are said to have less body odor than, say, Europeans or Arabs because few Japanese have apocrine glands.

Apocrine glands are sweat glands located under the arms, around the nipples, and in the pubic area. The secretion of these glands is in itself odorless, but it acquires a strong scent when it is decomposed by bacteria that live on the skin.

While most Europeans and Africans have apocrine glands, in 90 percent of Japanese the glands have receded, so the source of the odors has been cut off.

In the West, some people regard apocrine odors as sexy, so much so that they try to find partners who have as strong a smell as possible.

Q: Why do Japanese people walk so fast?

A: If you watch a marathon on television, you'll notice that the Japanese and people from other countries have very different strides when they run. The foreigners run three steps for every five of the Japanese.

It's the same when people walk. When Japanese walk

じ。外国人と並んで歩こうとすると、相手が3
歩あるくうちに、こちらは5歩もあるく必要が
ある。そのため、日本人の歩き方は、見るから
にせわしない。

　もちろん、このストライドの差は、脚の長さ
の違いによる。しかし、それだけでは説明しき
れない。

　足のつけ根にある腸骨大腿じん帯という部分
が、外国人に比べて日本人は短く、股関節の可
動範囲が小さいことも影響しているのである。

　わかりやすくいえば、股関節の柔軟性がない
から、脚が開かない。脚が開かないから、歩幅
が狭くなり、ちょこまかと歩いているように見
えるのである。

　ちなみに、カール・ルイスの走り方の特徴は、
股関節の柔らかさにある。日本でも、ビデオテ
ープで、カール・ルイスの走りを徹底研究し、
股関節の使い方を真似ようと努力しているが、
成功した人はいない。

　カール・ルイスは、日本人とは反対に、腸骨
大腿じん帯が長い典型的な選手だったといえる
だろう。

Q: なぜ、日本人はヘソの緒を保存するのか？

A: ───── 欧米人に、大事にとってあるヘソの緒を見せて
も、気味悪がられるだけだろう。欧米や中近東
の国では、そんな風習はまったく見かけられな
い。

side-by-side with foreigners, they have to take five steps to the foreigners' three. That's why the Japanese walking style seems so rushed and frantic.

One of the reasons, of course, is that our legs are shorter, but the length of legs does not explain everything.

Another factor is that Japanese have shorter iliofemoral ligaments, which connect the legs to the pelvis. As a result, Japanese hip joints have a narrower range of motion.

To put it more simply, Japanese hip joints have no flexibility, so the legs cannot be spread widely. Japanese people must take shorter strides, so they appear rushed and restless when they walk.

Carl Lewis's running style is marked by very flexible hip joints. Researchers in Japan have carefully studied his running style on videotape and tried to get runners to imitate the way he uses his hip joints, but without success.

Carl Lewis is a typical athlete with long iliofemoral ligaments—the opposite of Japanese runners.

Q: Why do Japanese mothers save their babies' umbilical cord?

A: If Japanese parents were to show a Westerner their baby's umbilical cord they had saved, the Westerner would likely feel disgusted. The custom of saving a piece of umbilical cord is completely unknown in Europe, America, and the Middle East.

日本人以外にヘソの緒を保存するのは、東南アジアの国ぐらい。たとえば、フィリピンでは、アルコール漬けにしてお守りにし、ラオスやインドネシアでは、土のなかに埋めて子供の成長を祈るという。

　東南アジアと日本は、意外なところで似ているが、もともとヘソの緒を保存するのは、母親と子供の絆を大切にすることから生まれた風習なのである。さらに、ヘソの緒が母親と子供の命をつなぐという神秘性から、特別な力があると信じられた。

　ここから、子供のお守りや成長を祈るおまじないとなったのである。

　じっさい、日本でも江戸時代には、ヘソの緒は長ければ長いほど長命につながると考えられていた。当時は、20〜30センチメートルのヘソの緒を保存していたという。

　また本人が大病をしたとき、煎じて飲めば、危急を救うとも伝えられていた。これも、ヘソの緒に、神秘的な力が宿っていると考えられていたためである。

　日本では、ヘソの緒が保存されていたことが、『日本書紀』にすでに記されている。

Q: なぜ、日本では特殊な泳法が発達したのか？

A:────── 現在の代表的な泳法というと、オリンピックに採用されているクロール、平泳ぎ、バタフライ、背泳ぎの4つになるだろう。しかし、日本人た

About the only people other than Japanese who save umbilical cords are Southeast Asians. In the Philippines, for example, the umbilical cords are immersed in alcohol and kept as good-luck charms. In Laos and Indonesia, people bury them in the ground and pray that the child will grow up healthy.

There are many surprising similarities between Southeast Asians and the Japanese. The custom of saving the umbilical cord originated as a way of cherishing the bond between mother and infant. It was also believed that this mysterious link between parent and child held some special power. The umbilical cord thus came to be regarded as an expression of the parents' prayers for the growth and safety of their children.

During the Edo period in Japan, it was thought that a longer umbilical cord would lead to a longer life, so cords twenty to thirty centimeters in length were sometimes saved. It was also believed that serious illnesses could be cured by having the patient drink a brew made from his or her umbilical cord. This is just another sign of the belief in the mystical powers of the umbilical cord.

Accounts of umbilical cords being saved in Japan can be found as early as the eighth-century *Nihon Shoki.*

Q: Why did a unique style of swimming develop in Japan?

A: The four main swimming strokes today are those used in the Olympics: the crawl, breaststroke, butterfly, and backstroke. We shouldn't forget, however, the swimming methods

るもの、日本泳法を忘れてはいけない。ときどき季節のニュースなどで目にする、あの優雅な泳ぎ方のことだ。

　足に扇子をはさんだり、泳ぎながら筆をもって字を書いたり、現在の私たちの目から見ると、優雅に水と戯れる、雅な泳法のように見える。しかし、そのルーツにはかなり血なまぐさいものがあるのだ。

　日本泳法のルーツは戦国時代にあり、もともとは戦闘技術として発達してきたものだ。

　鎧や刀をつけたままで、水中を移動する方法として考案され、体力を消耗しないよう、また敵に発見されないよう、さまざまな工夫が重ねられてきたのだ。

　それが、優雅な泳法に変身したのは、天下泰平の江戸時代。この時代に様式化がすすみ、現在の優雅な日本泳法ができあがった。現在残っている型は、おおむね江戸中期に完成したものだ。

　日本泳法には、平体、横体、立体の3つがあるが、これは水面に対する体のむきをさし、平体の代表は平泳ぎ、横体は伸しとも呼ばれる横泳ぎ、立体は立ち泳ぎがその代表だ。

　「犬かき」しかできない人も、嘆くなかれ。あの犬かきも、ルーツをたどれば、れっきとした「日本泳法」の1つだ。

developed by the Japanese. This is the graceful swimming style seen occasionally on seasonal news on television.

Holding a fan between their feet or writing with a brush as they swim, the swimmers appear to our modern eyes to be playing elegantly with the water. The roots of this swimming style, though, are much more gruesome.

Japanese swimming styles date back to the Sengoku, or Warring States, period of the fifteenth and fixteenth centuries. They originated as a method of fighting.

Techniques were developed for moving through water wearing armor and swords without tiring or being discovered by the enemy. These evolved into more graceful swimming styles during the Edo period, when Japan was at peace. The stylization of so many activities at that time led to the creation of the present elegant Japanese swimming style, which was perfected around the middle of the Edo period.

There are three basic styles—parallel, lateral, and perpendicular—according to the swimmer's orientation to the water surface. The parallel method is a breast stroke, while the lateral method includes a side stroke and the perpendicular method a kind of treading water.

Even if you can only dog-paddle, there's no need to be embarrassed. Dog-paddling, too, was originally a style of Japanese swimming.

第4章 日本「製品」の雑学

Q: なぜ、日本の即席メンは、世界中で食べられるようになったのか？

A: ────── 海外旅行みやげに即席メンを買ってくる人は多い。しかし、買った即席メンは、よく見ると、小さく「メイド・イン・ジャパン」と書いてあったりする。

現在、即席メンは、世界90ヵ国で年間130億食が出回っている。

そのうち、外国で消費される84億食の約70パーセントは、日本からの輸出か、海外の日系企業が販売したもの。それほど、日本の即席メンは世界中で食べられているのだ。

世界制覇まであと一歩の理由は、日本の企業がその国民の好みを徹底調査し、好みに合わせた即席メンを売りだしてきたからである。

もちろん、アジア各国のように、日本の醤油味がウケたケースもあるが、あるメーカーでは、たとえばアメリカでは、ビーフフレーバー、チキンフレーバー、ポークフレーバーの3種を用

CHAPTER 4
Trivia on
Japanese Products

Q: Why did Japanese instant noodles become popular around the world?

A: Many Japanese who travel overseas bring back instant noodles as souvenirs. If you inspect the packages of noodles that they buy, though, you'll often find "Made in Japan" printed in tiny type.

Each year, some 13 billion servings of instant noodles are sold in ninety countries worldwide. Of the 8.4 billion servings consumed outside Japan, about 70 percent are either imported from Japan or sold by Japanese companies located overseas. That shows how much Japanese instant noodles are eaten around the world.

The reason Japanese companies have nearly conquered the world with their noodles is that they carefully study the tastes of the people in each country and sell noodles that match those tastes.

Noodles with a soy sauce flavor have been popular in other Asian countries, of course. One manufacturer, though, developed three flavors for the United States: beef, chicken, and pork. That company had learned that Americans care

意。アメリカ人が舌の味わいより香りを優先することを知って、アメリカ人好みの3つの味を販売している。

しかも、天気のいい西海岸では、屋外で食べられるようにカップ入りが中心。反対に東海岸では、家庭で食べる袋入りを中心に販売。しっかり生活のなかにとけこんでいるのである。

また、欧米では、フォークでも扱いやすいようにメンを短くしているが、それが、同時に食べるさいのズルズルという音を防ぐ効果も計算してある。さらに、熱湯が苦手な人が多いため、ぬるい湯でもメンがほぐれるように工夫されている。

他国の即席メンのメーカーに、ここまで気を配っているところはないようだ。

Q: なぜ、日本のファクシミリは、世界を制することができたのか?

A: ──────── 世界中でつかわれている日本製品の1つに、ファクシミリがあるのをご存じだろうか。

現在、世界で、日本製のファクシミリが占めるシェアは、少なく見積もっても95パーセント。圧倒的な強さを誇っている。数年前まではほぼ100パーセントを達成していた。最近、値段の安い韓国製にやや押されて、少しシェアを下げたところだという。

もともとイギリスで発明されたファクシミリだが、日本製が世界を制したのは、日本語が特殊だったせいである。

more about the flavor than the taste on the tongue, so they offered three varieties with flavors that Americans like.

Instant noodles are adapted to match local lifestyles. On the West Coast of the U.S., where the weather is good, noodles are mainly sold in cups so that they can be eaten outdoors. On the East Coast, they are mostly sold in packets so that they can be cooked at home.

The noodles marketed in America and Europe are shorter. This not only allows them to be eaten more easily with a fork, it also helps to prevent slurping noises. And since many people there dislike hot water, the noodles are designed so they'll cook even in lukewarm water.

Non-Japanese manufacturers of instant noodles do not seem to give as much care to their products.

Q: Why did Japanese facsimile machines become a leading product in the world?

A: Did you know that one Japanese product that is used worldwide is the facsimile machine?

Japanese-made faxes now have over a 95 percent share of the global market. Their dominance is unrivaled. Until a few years ago the share was nearly 100 percent, but some inexpensive Korean-made faxes have recently managed to take a small bite out of the market.

The facsimile was invented in Britain, but Japan was able to capture the world market thanks to the unique nature of the Japanese writing system. Since Japanese is

漢字と仮名をつかう日本語は、文字が図形のように送れるファクシミリがピッタリだった。それに対して、アルファベットの欧米では、ファクシミリよりテレックスがむいていた。そのため、欧米のメーカーは、当初、ファクシミリの開発に興味を示さなかったのである。

　その間に、日本では、1972年、電電公社（現NTT）の回線が開放され、一般回線で利用できるようになった。これをきっかけに、メーカーが、いっせいに技術開発競争を展開。事務用ファクシミリが急速に普及し、90年ぐらいから、一般家庭にも広がっていった。同時に、世界市場でのシェアも、どんどん伸ばしていったのである。

　もちろん、その間、欧米のメーカーも、文字しか送れないテレックスに比べ、図形の送れるファクシミリを見直したが、時すでに遅し。日本のメーカーとの技術力の差は、埋められなかったのである。

　現在、世界市場では、日韓に台湾も加えたファクシミリの売りこみ戦争が繰り広げられている。

Q: 日本では、なぜ漆器が発達したのか？

A: ───────ジャパンという英語には、日本という意味のほかに「漆器」という意味もある。イギリス人には、チャイナの陶器に対して、日本の漆器のイメージが強烈だったのだが、これほど日本に漆器が発達したのは、日本人が味噌汁を中心とした熱い"スープ"が好きだからといえる。

written with both *kanji* and *kana* characters, the fax was an ideal method for sending Japanese text as images. The telex was better suited for European languages that are alphabet-based. For that reason, Western manufacturers had no interest in developing facsimiles at first.

In 1972, the Nippon Telegraph and Telephone Public Corporation—now the private company NTT—opened up its circuits for anyone to use. That move led manufacturers into a fierce competition to develop new technology. Facsimiles for business use soon become popular, and around 1990 faxes began to be used in homes as well. At the same time, Japan's share of the global market grew steadily.

Western manufacturers took a new look at facsimiles when they realized that, unlike telex machines, faxes could send not only text but also images, but by then it was too late. They couldn't catch up with the technical level of the Japanese manufacturers.

The world market for faxes is now developing into a three-way competition among Japan, Korea, and Taiwan.

Q: Why was lacquerware developed in Japan?

A: The English word "Japan" refers not only to the country but also to the lacquerware. Japanese lacquer made as strong an impression on the British as did Chinese ceramics. The reason lacquerware was developed in Japan is due to the Japanese love for *miso* and other hot soups.

　もともと木製の器は、熱い汁物を入れるのに適している。木が熱を伝えないから、なかのものがさめにくいのである。

　ところが木製の器は、生地だけでは汚れやすく、また割れやすいという欠点がある。それらを防止するために、漆を塗って工夫された。日本で漆器が発達したのは、そのためである。

　漆器は、まず器に下塗りをし、乾くと布をはる。そこへ砥の粉を塗り、もう一度漆を塗る。ここまでが下地づくりで、その後、上塗りして乾かし、乾かして上塗りする作業を繰り返し、やっと割れない器ができあがる。

　また、何度も漆を上塗りした器だから、その上、絵や模様を自由に描くことができた。蒔絵や、色漆でさまざまな模様をつけたもの、なかを真っ赤に塗った根来塗りなど、芸術的にも高い評価を受けるようになった。

Q: なぜ、日本の杯は平たいのか？

A: ————外国で、いろいろなパーティに招かれたという人も多いだろう。人が集まっているのでいってみると、結婚披露宴。砂漠の国のらくだの丸焼きなど、現地の縁起物料理をご馳走になるなんてことも、旅の楽しみの一つである。

　そんな宴会に入れてもらって気がつくのは、日本の杯の珍しさ。どの国でも宴会に酒はつきものだが、ほとんどの国で、酒を飲むときの器は、コップ状のものかボウル状のもの。日本の

Wooden containers are good for holding hot liquids. Since wood does not conduct heat well, it keeps the contents from cooling.

However, wood has its problems. If left uncoated, it gets dirty and cracks easily. To prevent that, techniques were invented for coating the wood with lacquer. That's how lacquerware came to be developed in Japan.

Lacquerware is made by first applying a primer coat to the wood and allowing it to dry. Then a layer of cloth is spread over the surface and this is coated with abrasive powder. Another coat of lacquer is applied to complete this base layer. Then more coats of lacquer are added and allowed to dry to create a tough, unbreakable piece.

Because the vessel has so many layers of varnish, pictures and patterns can be drawn on it. The prized artistry of lacquerware comes in many styles, including *maki-e* (sprinkled pictures), *iro-urushi* (colored lacquer), and the bright crimson *Negoro-nuri* (Negoro lacquer).

Q: Why are traditional Japanese saké cups shallow?

A: People traveling abroad are often invited to parties. Whether the gathering is a wedding reception or a camel roast in the desert, the chance to enjoy a local feast is one of the pleasures of traveling.

A Japanese person invited to a celebration overseas is likely to notice how unusual Japanese wine cups are. Wine accompanies banquets everywhere, and in most countries the wine is drunk out of deep vessels shaped like glasses or

杯のように、平たい器で酒を飲むところはほとんどない。

　よく考えてみれば、平たい器は入る量が少ない。酒好きには、じれったい器でもあるが、日本の杯は、その昔、貝殻で酒を飲んでいたときの名残だという。

　四方を海で囲まれた日本では、もともと、貝殻で酒を飲んでいた。

　そのため、土器をつかうようになっても、酒器は、底が浅く平たいものをつかい続けたのである。

　ちなみに、中国からヨーロッパにかけては、もともと動物の角で酒を飲んでいた。それが、土器になると、底がとがっていたり丸くなっている尖底土器となり、ここからいまのコップが生まれている。

Q: なぜ、日本人がアロハシャツを発明したのか？

A: ──────── ハワイで、アロハシャツを買ってくる人は多い。ところが、ハワイにいってみると、アロハシャツを着ている人は、ハワイアン・バンドのオニイサンぐらいしか発見できない。

　いまや、現地の人も着ないアロハシャツを、なぜ日本人が好きなのかと思ったら、もともと、アロハシャツをつくったのは、日本人だったという。

　その日本人とは、ハワイ移民第一世代の宮本孝一郎さんである。宮本さんは、ハワイで「武蔵屋」という着物屋を営んでいた。昭和8年（1933年）のある日、その店に、1人の白人客があらわれ、こう注文した。

bowls. Almost nowhere do people drink wine from flat cups like in Japan.

Flat containers can't hold much wine, of course, so wine lovers are likely to get impatient with them. Japanese wine cups are said to be based on the ancient tradition of drinking wine from sea shells. Since Japan is surrounded on all sides by ocean, that was the way wine was originally consumed. Even after people began using earthenware vessels, they continued to drink wine from flat-bottomed containers.

In Eurasia, people originally drank from animal horns. When they switched to earthenware, they continued to use round vessels with pointed bottoms. That was the origin of the deep-bottomed glass.

Q: Why did a Japanese man invent the aloha shirt?

A: Many Japanese tourists come back from Hawaii with aloha shirts. In Hawaii, though, about the only people you'll see wearing those colorful garments are the musicians in Hawaiian bands.

The reason Japanese people like those shirts—even though they aren't worn by people in Hawaii—is that Hawaiian shirts were invented by a Japanese man.

His name was Miyamoto Kōichiro. A first-generation immigrant to Hawaii, Miyamoto ran a kimono shop there called Musashiya. One day in 1933, a Caucasian man came to his store and made the following request.

「日本のゆかたは、カラフルできれいだから、それでシャツをつくってほしい」それならおやすいご用と、宮本さんがつくりあげたのが、世界最初のアロハシャツだった。つまり、アロハシャツのルーツは、ゆかた。どうりで、日本人観光客に、人気が高いわけである。

Q: 「別れのテープ」は、なぜ日本人が発明したのか？

A: ———— 赤や青など色とりどりの紙テープを投げて、別れを惜しむ。この船の別れのシーンは、世界中で行われているが、もともと「別れのテープ」を発明したのが日本人だということは、あまり知られていない。

このアイデアを思いついたのは、森田庄吉という人。もちろん、紙テープの商人である。

1915年（大正4年）森田さんは、前年のパナマ運河の開通を記念して、サンフランシスコで開かれた万国博覧会に出品。包装用の紙テープを展示した。ところが、さっぱり売れない。大量の在庫をかかえて呆然とする森田さんだったが、ふと名案が浮かんだ。

残った紙テープを港にもっていき、「テープで別れの握手」というキャッチフレーズで売りだしたのである。たちまち大人気となり、あっという間に世界中に広まった。現在では、紙テープで海が汚れると禁止するところもあるが、苦しまぎれのアイデアが、世界の別れのドラマを盛り上げることになった。

"Those Japanese cotton robes are really colorful and attractive. I'd like you to make a shirt for me from the same cloth."

It was as easily said as done, and what Miyamoto made for his customer became the world's first aloha shirt. Thus the Hawaiian shirt originated from the *yukata*. And that's why the shirts are so popular with Japanese tourists.

Q: Why did a Japanese invent farewell streamers for ships?

A: Images of people on ships throwing colorful red and blue paper streamers in sad farewell can be seen throughout the world, but few people know that the inventor of paper streamers was Japanese.

The man who thought up the idea was named Morita Shōkichi. Not surprisingly, he was in the paper tape business.

In 1915, Morita exhibited some of his wrapping tape at the Panama-Pacific International Exposition, which was held in San Francisco in honor of the opening of the Panama Canal the previous year. Sales were terrible. Morita was at a loss over what to do about his huge inventory. But then he had a great idea.

He took his leftover tape down to the harbor and began selling it with the slogan, "Say Good-bye with Tape." It soon became popular, and in no time at all the practice spread around the world. Although in some places the streamers are now banned because they litter the ocean, the idea that came to Morita in desperation has added drama and excitement to farewells throughout the world.

Q: 日本のノコギリは、なぜ引いてつかうのか？

A: ──────欧米人が、日本のノコギリをつかっているところを見ると、「なにを考えているの？」と首をひねるそうだ。欧米のノコギリは、押して切るのに、日本のノコギリは、引いて切る。

欧米人は、日本のノコギリは、刃が自分のほうをむいて危ないと感じるらしい。しかし、引いてつかうノコギリは、アジア諸国でもつかわれている。このアジア式の引いてつかうノコギリは、床や地面にあぐらをかいて作業するのにピッタリなのである。

じっさいあぐらをかいて作業すると、ノコギリは引くほうがつかいやすく、疲れない。しかも、細かい作業には、だんぜん手元に引いて切るノコギリのほうが適している。刃が曲がる心配がなく、薄いものでも切りやすいし、切り口がゆがみにくいからである。

そのため、試しにつかってみると、引いてつかう日本式のノコギリのほうが便利だという欧米人も多い。

「なにを考えているの？」と首をひねっていた人が、喜んでもち帰ったりもするという。

Q: 日本の浮世絵は、なぜ外国に広まったのか？

A: ──────日本の浮世絵は、名品の多くが海外に流出してしまっている。いまになって、海外から買い戻しているが、もともと外国に出ていったのは、ヨー

Q: Why do Japanese hand saws cut while being pulled?

A: Many Westerners shake their heads in wonder when they see Japanese using hand saws. The reason is that Japanese saws cut on the pull stroke. In the West, saws cut while being pushed.

Westerners seem to think that Japanese saws are dangerous because the teeth face toward the operator. But the pull saw is used not only in Japan but in other Asian countries as well. The reason is that the pull saw is ideal when the worker is sitting cross-legged on the floor or ground.

If you try to saw while sitting cross-legged, it's much easier and less tiring to pull the saw rather than to push it. Pull-saws are also much better for delicate work. You don't have to worry about the blade buckling, it's easy to cut thin pieces, and the cut groove stays straighter.

Many Westerners who try using Japanese pull-saws say that they are actually more convenient.

So the Westerners who shook their heads in wonder when they first saw Japanese saws are often happy to take some of the tools back home.

Q: Why did *ukiyo-e* become popular in other countries?

A: Many great works of *ukiyo-e* woodblock prints wound up in other countries. Some have since been bought back by the Japanese. However, the reason many of the prints originally

ロッパ人が買い求めたからだけではなかった。

江戸時代、ヨーロッパの人々には、むしろ、有田焼や九谷焼といった焼き物のほうが人気だった。彼らは、日本から陶芸品をどんどん買いつけたが、届いた焼き物の包みを開いて驚いた。

焼き物を包む紙に、美しい版画が刷りこんであったからである。つまり、浮世絵がヨーロッパに渡ったのは、まず焼き物をつつむ包装紙としてだったのである。

「なぜ、そんなもったいないことを」と思うのは、いまの感覚。当時の江戸で、浮世絵は一種の流行品。役者絵や風俗絵など、出るたびに買い換え、流行がすたれれば、古いものは捨てていた。

ただし、紙は貴重品だったから、たまたま焼き物の包み紙として再利用されたというわけである。

やがて、ヨーロッパでは、焼き物以上に、浮世絵の人気が高まった。それから、大量に買い求めるようになったのである。

画家のゴッホも、浮世絵を愛したことで知られているが、パリには浮世絵を売る店が何軒も開かれたことがあるという。

Q: 日本の階段は、なぜ、急傾斜で狭いのか？

A: ————— 日本のお城の階段は、どこも急傾斜で狭い。団体さんといっしょになると、なかなか前にすすめなくなるが、お城の階段が不便なのは、もともと生活のための階段ではなかったからである。

left Japan is not that they were bought by Europeans.

During the Edo period, Europeans were more interested in Japanese ceramics like Arita and Kutani ware and ordered many ceramic pieces from Japan. When the ceramics arrived and the buyers opened the wrappings, they found something inside that surprised them. The earthenware was wrapped in beautiful woodblock prints. The first *ukiyo-e* to reach Europe arrived as wrapping paper for ceramics.

Today we are shocked by the waste. In the Edo period, though, *ukiyo-e* were just another fad. The pictures of actors and night-life districts were bought as soon as they came out, and when the fashions changed the old pictures would be thrown away.

In those days, paper was a valuable commodity, so the prints would sometimes be reused as wrapping paper for ceramics.

In Europe, the prints eventually became more popular than the ceramics, and people began buying them in large quantities.

Van Gogh liked *ukiyo-e*, and there were several stores in Paris that sold the prints.

Q: Why are Japanese staircases so steep and narrow?

A: All staircases in Japanese castles are steep and narrow. If you get stuck behind a tour group, you won't be able to move forward. The reason that stairs in castles are so cramped is that they were never intended for daily use.

お城の階段を上がっていくと、天守閣に通じる。だが、この天守閣は、人々の生活の場ではなかった。じつは、非常の場合に逃げこむ場所だったのである。敵が攻めてくると、天守閣にこもり、階段を切り落とした。

そのため、敵が上がってこないように、急傾斜で狭い階段にする必要があったのである。さらに、階段は、できるだけ人目につかないところにつけられるのがふつうだった。

この建築は、日本の一般家屋にも受け継がれていった。昔の家の階段は、たいてい狭くて急傾斜。映画でみる欧米の家のように、踊り場があったり曲がったりしていない。

昔の日本で、2階は生活の場というより、遊びとか、お客用とかいった、非日常の空間だった。階段は、日常と非日常をつなぐもの。かならずしも便利であることは求められなかったのである。

Q: 日本のカゼ薬は、なぜ効き目が弱いのか？

A: ──────── 外国で、カゼ薬の効き目のよさにビックリすることがある。旅先で、すすめられて外国製のカゼ薬を飲んだら、翌日にはスッキリ。のどの痛みなどの症状が、すっかり消えているということがある。

こんな体験を一度でもすると、日本のカゼ薬は、なんと甘っちょろいのかと思ってしまうが、日本のカゼ薬の効き目がいまひとつなのは、安全第一に製造されているからだという。

Castle stairs lead to the tower, and in the old days nobody lived up there. The tower was only used for refuge in case of emergencies. When attacked, the people in the castle would retreat into the tower and block off the staircase.

To stop the enemy from coming up, the staircases had to be steep and narrow. The stairs were also usually built in places where they wouldn't be noticed.

That style of construction was adopted in regular homes in Japan as well. In the old days, most staircases in houses were steep. None had landings or curves like the stairs seen in American and European movies.

The second floors of Japanese homes were not primarily for living. They were special areas used for recreation or guests. The staircase was a link between daily life below and special occasions above, so there was no reason for them to be easy to use.

Q: Why is Japanese cold medicine so ineffective?

A: Japanese living overseas are often surprised at the effectiveness of cold medicines there. When given some foreign medication while traveling, they find they are completely recovered by the next day, their sore throats and other symptoms gone.

A single experience like that makes Japanese cold medicine seem ineffective. The reason it is so is because top priority is given to safety.

たとえば、薬はつかわれている成分の量が、日本とアメリカでは、ずいぶん違う。だいたい、日本の薬物の使用量は、アメリカの80パーセント以下。成分によっては、50パーセント以下となっている。アスピリンなど、アメリカの制限は1日最大4,000ミリグラムだが、日本では1,500ミリグラムに抑えられている。飲む量が違えば、効き目に差が出て当然なのである。

また、日本のカゼ薬は、ほとんど総合感冒薬。外国の薬が、のどの痛み、鼻づまり、熱など症状に合わせたものなのに、日本では、いろいろな成分を混ぜ合わせ、症状に関係なく服用するようになっている。

「より多くの成分が入っているほうが、効果が高そうで、お得」と思うのか、日本では、総合感冒薬の人気が高いからだが、そのために、一つ一つの症状に対する効き目が、いまひとつ弱くなってしまうのである。

アメリカで、総合感冒薬は、「ヘタな鉄砲も数撃ちゃ当たる」式の薬と思われ、まったく人気がない。

Q: 日本は、なぜ新聞普及率が世界一なのか？

A: ──────── 若者の新聞ばなれがすすんでいるといっても、日本の新聞普及率は、世界でナンバーワン。人口の1,000人あたり500部をこえ、断トツ1位である。

この新聞普及率を支えているのは、宅配制度である。

The quantities of the ingredients used in medicine are very different between Japan and the United States. The amounts used in Japanese medicines are generally at most 80 percent of the American quantities, sometimes only 50 percent or even less. The daily limit for aspirin intake is 4,000 milligrams in the U.S. but only 1,500 milligrams in Japan. Not surprisingly, less medicine means less effect.

Almost all cold remedies sold in Japan are of the general-purpose type, while medicines in other countries are usually directed at a specific symptom such as sore throat, nasal congestion, or fever. In Japan, cold sufferers take a combination of different medicines regardless of their specific symptoms.

General-purpose medicines may be more popular in Japan because a medication that contains a variety of components seems more effective and a better bargain. The result, though, is that the actual effect on individual symptoms is weaker.

In the U.S., general-purpose nostrums are regarded as a scattershot method of targeting illnesses, so few people use them.

Q: Why does Japan have the largest newspaper readership in the world?

A: Although it is said that young people in Japan do not read newspapers, the country's overall rate of newspaper readership is still far and away the highest in the world. More than 500 copies are sold for every 1,000 people.

The reason for Japan's high readership rate is an efficient system of home delivery. When people wake up in

朝起きれば家のポストに新聞が入っていて、夕方帰ってくると夕刊が配られている。しかも全国的に、これだけしっかりした宅配制度をもっているのは、日本ぐらいである。

多くの国で、宅配はあっても一部の地域のみ。たいていの人は、駅や町の売店で買う。日本も、もし売店で買うシステムなら、新聞はこれほど普及していないはずである。

ただし、宅配制度で大変なのが配達人の確保。主婦や学生が中心だが、毎日、しかも天気に関係なく、朝の5時ぐらいから配達となると、なり手は少ない。

自立志向の学生が、住みこんで配達しているケースが多いが、アルバイト感覚の学生や高校生のなかには、当日の朝、「今日は休みます」と連絡を入れてきて、販売店のオーナーを激怒させる困ったヤツも増えているという。

Q: 日本には、なぜこんなにも喫茶店が多いのか？

A: ──────「江戸に多きものは稲荷、伊勢屋に犬のフン」とは、江戸の町にあふれていたものだが、いまの東京に多いのが、カラオケと喫茶店である。

カラオケ店は、日本が発祥の地。多くて当たり前だが、喫茶店の数は、カラオケ店以上だ。

昔から茶店があったといっても、茶店は、旅人相手の商売。外国と比較しても、日本には、喫茶店が異常に多い。

その1つの理由は、家やオフィスが互いに遠

the morning, they find the newspaper in their mail box; when they come home at night, the evening edition is waiting. Japan is privileged to have such a reliable, nation-wide system for delivering newspapers.

In some countries, home delivery is not made to every house, and people have to buy newspapers at train stations or local shops. If newspapers were available only at stores in Japan, they would probably not be so popular.

The difficult part about home delivery, though, is hir-ing enough delivery people, most of whom are housewives or students. Few people want to deliver newspapers at five o'clock every morning regardless of the weather.

Often students who want to be independent of their parents live in rooms provided by the delivery agents they work for. Recently, though, many high-school and college students regard the work as just another part-time job, and they're more likely to call in the morning to say that they are taking the day off. This makes the delivery agents furious.

Q: Why are there so many coffee shops in Japan?

A: In old Edo, it used to be said that anywhere you looked you'd find *inari*, *iseya*, and *inu no fun*, which might be translated roughly as "shrines, shops, and dog shit." In today's Tokyo, those ubiquities have been replaced by karaoke and coffee shops.

Karaoke was invented in Japan, so it's no wonder there are many karaoke places. But the number of cafés is even greater.

In earlier eras Japan had tea shops, but they were only

くて狭いことにある。たとえば、欧米で、お茶の時間といえば、誰かの家に集まるのがふつうである。

ところが、日本では、通勤圏や通学圏が広く、家が遠い。たとえ近くても、家が狭く、つい喫茶店を利用することになる。

オフィスでも事情は同じ。ちょっと打ち合わせをしようとしても、会議室や応接室の数が少ない。

あぶれた人は、喫茶店をつかうことになる。つまり、家やオフィスの欠点を喫茶店は補っているのである。

また、喫茶店の多さは、日本人が小金をもっていることの証明でもある。

よその国には、ヒマをつぶすためにカフェにいくという人は少ない。コーヒーや紅茶を頼めば、よけいな出費をするからである。

友人同士のおしゃべりでも、喫茶店より公園などへいくことが多い。無駄なお金は、できるだけつかわないのがふつうなのだ。

日本では、大学生でも、ヒマがあれば喫茶店に入って数百円をつかう。これを毎日続けるのは、さすがに小金をもっていないとできることではない。

for travelers. Today the number of cafés—or *kissaten*—is much higher than in other countries.

One reason is that homes and offices are small and far away. In Europe or America, people are likely to gather for tea in someone's home. In Japan, people travel longer distances to work and to school, and their homes are small. Even if people live near each other, they are more likely to go to a coffee shop than to someone's cramped residence.

The situation in offices is the same. Most offices in Japan don't have enough meeting or reception rooms for casual gatherings.

As a result, people use coffee shops as meeting spots. Those establishments make up for the lack of room in homes and offices.

The large number of cafés is also proof that the Japanese always carry extra cash.

In other countries, few people go to a coffee shop just to kill time, because ordering a coffee or tea would be a needless expense.

If friends want to talk, they're more likely to go to a park than a café, because people do not like to waste money.

In Japan, even college students with a little free time will go into a coffee shop and spend a few hundred yen. If they didn't have the extra cash available, they would not be able to do this on a daily basis.

第5章 日本の「伝統」の雑学

Q: 日本人は、なぜお中元を贈るようになったのか？

A: ──────お中元というと、百貨店に足を運ぶ人が多い。「進物には百貨店の包み紙がふさわしい」という一種のブランド信仰があるためだろうが、もともとお中元と百貨店は切っても切れない関係にあったといえるのだ。

現在の「お中元」は、じつは百貨店の販売戦略が生みだしたものなのだ。明治44年（1911年）、三越呉服店は、こんな広告を打った。

「中元来れり、中元来れり。お盆の御つかいものは、東京なる三越呉服店へご注文あそばされなば早速御届け申上ぐべし」
　要するに「お盆の進物は、うちでどうぞ」というCMだ。この明治末のサマーセールは大当たりをとり、それならばとほかの百貨店も追随し、あっという間に夏の贈り物を「お中元」と呼ぶことが定着した。
　もっとも、「中元」という言葉は昔からあっ

CHAPTER 5

Trivia on Japanese Traditions

Q: Why do the Japanese send each other gifts at midsummer?

A: When it's time to buy midsummer presents—*o-chūgen*—many people go to department stores. Part of the reason is the obsession with brand names, and a department store's wrapping paper is seen as appropriate for gifts. The original reason, though, is the intimate connection between department stores and midsummer gifts.

In fact, the *o-chūgen* custom as we know it today arose from a department store's marketing strategy. In 1911, the Mitsukoshi Department Store released the following advertisement:

"Midsummer [*chūgen*] is here, midsummer is here.
If you order what you need for *o-bon* at Mitsukoshi
in Tokyo, we will deliver it promptly."

It was a commercial asking people to shop at Mitsukoshi for their gifts for *o-bon*, the summer festival in honor of ancestors. The ad for Mitsukoshi's summer sale was a big success, so other department stores copied it. Soon everyone was calling midsummer gifts *o-chūgen*.

The word *chūgen* dates back much earlier. The same

た。もともとは、中国の道教の教典である『真書』にある言葉で、1月15日が上元の日、7月15日を中元の日、10月15日を下元の日と呼んだことが、この言葉のはじまりだ。

　これが日本に入り、江戸時代、徳川幕府は、ほぼ1年の真ん中にあたる「中元」に目をつけて、特別のあいさつを交わす日に定めた。この日は、大名が白装束（しろしょうぞく）で登城（とじょう）して将軍に拝謁（はいえつ）したりした。

　一方、それとは別に、庶民のあいだでは、7月15日、つまりお盆に、多少の贈り物を交換する習慣があった。三越呉服店は、これらをうまく組み合わせて、「中元の贈り物」という習慣を日本人のあいだに浸透させたわけだ。

Q: 日本人は、端午の節句に、なぜ鯉のぼりを立てるのか？

A: ─────── 大都市では、年々、端午（たんご）の節句（5月5日）に立てる鯉のぼりの数が少なくなっている。立てる場所がないというのが一番の理由だろうが、ちょっと寂しい気分になる。

　鯉のぼりは初夏の風物詩だが、もともと、この鯉のぼり、中国の悲しい逸話がもとになっている。

　昔、中国の楚（そ）の国で、屈原（くつげん）という人物（政治家・詩人）が批判されて、汨羅江（べきらこう）の淵に身を投げて死んでしまった。

　この屈原を哀れに思った楚の人が、紙の鯉をつくって祀（まつ）ったのである。

characters are found in a Chinese Taoist text called *Zhenshu*. The *kanji* used for *chūgen* literally mean "middle source," and they refer to July 15. That day was associated with January 15, which was called "top source," and October 15, or "bottom source."

These terms were adopted in Japan, and during the Edo period the Tokugawa shogunate decided to make *chūgen* a time for exchanging special greetings because it came close to the middle of the year. On that day, the regional bigwigs would dress all in white to go and pay their respects to the shogun at his castle.

The common people at that time had a separate custom of exchanging *o-bon* presents on July 15. The Mitsukoshi Department Store cleverly combined those practices to establish a new custom among Japanese of giving presents at midsummer.

Q: Why do the Japanese fly carp streamers during Boys' Festival?

A: In recent years, fewer carp streamers are displayed in big cities during Boys' Festival on May 5 mainly because there is no place to put them. Many people miss seeing the colorful decorations.

Carp streamers are a symbol of early summer, but they originated in a sad tale from China.

Long ago, in the Chinese kingdom of Chu, a politician and poet named Qu Yuan was criticized so strongly that he threw himself into Lake Miluo and died. The people of Chu mourned Qu Yuan by hanging a paper carp that they had made.

それが日本にも伝わり、室町時代に、武士の家で、長い布を半月形にたわめた竹に張って竿につけ、ちょうど戦いのときののぼりのような吹き流しを立てるようになった。優秀で人望の厚かった屈原のように、男の子の立身出世を願って立てたのである。

　さらに江戸時代になると、武士だけでなく町家でも、紙でつくった鯉を竿頭に揚げるようになった。これを「五月鯉」と呼んだが、屈原のエピソードに、「鯉の滝のぼり」で知られるように威勢がよい鯉のイメージが重なって、男の子の健康を願う端午の節句の行事になったのである。

　もともと端午の節句は旧暦の最初の午の日、つまり、端午の日を祝ったものだったが、いつからか、5月5日に祝うようになった。5月5日が子供の日として祝日になったのは、戦後のことである。

Q: 日本人は、なぜ引っ越しそばを食べるのか？

A: ──────── 引っ越ししてくると近所にそばを配るという習慣は、もともと都市部ではじまったものである。

　「そばのように末長く、あなたのそばで暮らしたい」「おそばに参りました」というゴロ合わせもあるようだが、その前は、餅を配るのが一般的だった。

　さらに、もっと昔は、近所の人を呼んで、いっ

This custom spread to Japan. In the Muromachi period, people in samurai households would attach long pieces of cloth in a half-moon shape on bamboo poles and hang them. The cloth flapped in the wind like battle flags. The flags showed the parents' hope that their sons would grow up to be successful, just like the talented and respected Qu Yuan.

In the Edo period, merchants as well as samurai adopted the custom of hanging paper carp from poles. The streamers were called "May Carp." The story of Qu Yuan became mixed with the image of a vigorous carp ascending a waterfall, and the streamers became a regular part of the May festival during which people prayed for the health of their sons.

The Japanese name for the festival, Tango no Sekku, literally referred to the first day of the old calendar year designated by the character *ushi*, which is also pronounced *go*. Since *go* is also the word for "five," the Boys' Festival came to be celebrated on the fifth day of the fifth month. After World War II, that day was designated a national holiday and is now called Children's Day.

Q: Why do the Japanese eat *soba* when they first move to a new home?

A: The custom of handing out dry *soba* noodles to neighbors after moving to a new home began in cities. The custom is partly a pun, as *soba* also means "nearby" or "next to." People might say, "Just as *soba* [noodles] are long, we want to live *anata no soba* [near you] for a long time," or "We have moved *o-soba* [near you]." Earlier, the custom was to give away *mochi*, or rice cakes.

And even earlier than that, the newcomers would invite

しょに食事をするのが習わしだった。現在の引っ越しそばを配るという習慣は、じつは近所の人と食事をともにしたことに由来するのである。

遠い親戚より、近くの他人という言葉があるように、日本社会では地域の結びつきが強い。引っ越してきた人が、その地域へ入っていくには、セレモニーが必要だったのである。

現在でも農村には残っているが、昔は、そのセレモニーが、いっしょに酒を飲み、食事をすることであった。盃をかわして、同じものを食べることで、仲間に入ることを許されたのである。

しかし、地縁が薄れてきた都市では、このセレモニーが簡略化され、やがて餅を配るようになり、さらに餅では手間がかかるからとそばを配るようになったのである。

Q: 日本では、なぜ紅白がおめでたくて、黒白がめでたくないのか？

A: ──────── 嫁入り道具を運ぶトラックには、紅白の幕。葬式には黒白の幕が張られるように、日本では紅白がおめでたく黒白がめでたくないものとなっている。そのルーツは、じつに上代以前にさかのぼるという。

そのころ、赤は明るさ、繁栄、まごころを示す色とされ、黒は、罪や汚れ、暗黒、希望がないということを示す色とされていた。おそらく、赤＝太陽、黒＝夜から、そういうイメージが生まれたのだろうと考えられる。

their neighbors over to eat together. Thus the custom of giving *soba* noodles comes from the tradition of eating together with one's new neighbors.

A Japanese proverb says that nearby strangers are more important than distant relatives. This shows the strength of local bonds in Japanese society. Those bonds required that newcomers be welcomed into a neighborhood with some kind of ceremony.

Such ceremonies, which still exist in rural villages, involve drinking and eating together. By passing around the wine cup and sharing food, the new arrivals are permitted to join the community.

In urban areas, where local ties have grown weaker, the ceremonies were simplified into the distribution of *mochi*. When even *mochi* became too much of a bother, people started giving away dried *soba*.

Q: Why are red and white auspicious colors but black and white are not?

A: The trucks that delivers the furniture of newlyweds to their new home are draped in red and white bunting. The curtains at funerals are colored black and white. In Japan, red and white are auspicious while black and white are not. The roots of this distinction stretch back even earlier than the Nara period.

In those days, red symbolized brightness, prosperity, and sincerity, while black represented sin, filth, darkness, and despair. Those images probably came from associating red with the sun and black with night.

その後の奈良時代には、赤い雲や赤い鳥は、良いことの兆し（きざ）ともされていた。しかし、この時代には、まだ、赤にめでたい、黒にめでたくないの区別はなかった。その傾向がはっきりしてきたのは、平安時代になってからである。

たとえば、『源氏物語』に、凶服（喪服のこと）として「鈍色（にびいろ）（薄墨色）の御衣（おんぞ）」という表現がある。また、『栄華物語』にも、「椎柴染（しいしばぞめ）の衣」という表現が出てくる。椎柴とは、椎の木の小枝を染料とした墨色の喪服ことである。平安時代から、赤が祥瑞（しょうずい）（めでたいの意）、黒が喪の意味をあらわすようになったようだ。

これが江戸時代になって、宮中儀礼のなかで、壁代幕（かべしろまく）（壁として室内のしきりにかけた布の幕）や几帳（きちょう）（室内をしきるために布をかけたもの）としてつかわれるようになった。やがて、この宮中儀礼が一般に広まり、現在のような幕となった。

張りめぐらすだけで、場の雰囲気を一気に変える紅白や黒白の幕には、やはり並々ならぬ年季が隠されているのである。

Q: なぜ、日本ではサインが普及しないのか？

A: ─────── ハンコ社会である日本では、出生届にはじまり、銀行口座の開設、書留の認め印、結婚届、離婚届、死亡届に至るまで、ハンコが必要となる。まさに、1人の人間が生きていることを証明するためには、ハンコが不可欠の世の中だ。

しかし、ハンコというのは、ときにわずらわ

In the Nara period, red clouds and red birds were taken to be signs of good luck, but the distinction between red as good and black as bad did not yet exist. That attitude first became established during the Heian period.

In *The Tale of Genji*, for example, the expression *nibiiro no onzo*, or "clothing of a pale charcoal color," describes mourning clothes, and *The Tale of the Flowering Fortunes* includes the term *shīshibazome* to describe a funeral garment (*shīshiba* refers to a black dye obtained from the branches of the chinquapin tree.) Since the Heian period, red has been the color of celebration and black the color of mourning.

In the Edo period, buntings with these colors began to be used in palace ceremonies as partition walls or they were draped over movable partitions. The custom eventually spread to the general population and became the colored drapes used today.

Bunting can instantly change the mood of a room. The red-and-white and black-and-white patterns used in ceremonies have a long and unique history in Japan.

Q: Why don't the Japanese use signatures for official purposes?

A: Japan is a country of signature seals. Personal seals called *hanko* are needed for practically everything, from opening bank accounts and receiving registered mail to signing birth, marriage, divorce, and death certificates. You practically need a *hanko* to prove that you exist.

But seals can also be a bother. Losing one creates a lot

しい代物で、紛失してはまずいし、かといって役所や銀行に出かけるのに、ハンコをもちださないわけにはいかない。

整理整頓の下手な人は、必要なときにハンコのしまい場所がわからず、毎回、「あれ？　ハンコはどこへしまったっけ？」と大騒ぎになる。欧米のようにハンコの代わりに自筆のサインを用いれば、ずいぶんラクだと思うのだが……。

じつは日本でも、サインを用いていた時代があった。平安時代の末期、「花押」と呼ばれる自筆のサインが公文書用の正式なものとして採用されていたのだ。しかし、これが欧米のサインと違ったところは、簡単には書けなかったことだ。

芸能人のサインのようにサラサラと書くものではなく、1つの花押を記すのにも、多大な時間と集中力を要した。いまも、歴代の閣僚が天皇陛下に奏上する閣議書には、この花押を書く習慣があるが、一般的につかわれることはない。

日本でサインが発達しなかったのは、日本式サインの原型であるこの花押が、ハンコを押すよりもさらにめんどうだったために、江戸時代に花押そのものがハンコになったからだと考えられている。

Q: 日本人は、なぜ旅先でお土産を買って帰るのか？

A: ──────海外旅行先で、丸一日をお土産選びに費やす人もいる。日本人のお土産好きは、いまや世界中に有名だが、「お土産」と書くので、その「土

of trouble, and you have to have one ready whenever you go to a government office or a bank.

Messy people can never find their *hanko* when they need it, and they make a big fuss trying to find it. Would is not be much easier just to use signatures as in the West?

In fact, there was a time when signatures were used in Japan. Toward the end of the Heian period, a kind of signature called a *kaō* was adopted for official documents. Unlike Western signatures, though, the *kaō* could not be written easily.

Today Japanese celebrities learn to sign their names quickly and with a flourish, but the people who signed their names with *kaō* expended much more time and concentration on them. Cabinet members still use *kaō* for the documents they submit to the Emperor. Otherwise, though, *kaō* are not widely used.

It seems that the reason signatures did not become more popular in Japan is that *kaō*, instead of developing into more informal signatures, were replaced in the Edo period by the much less time-consuming *hanko*.

Q: Why do the Japanese always bring back gifts from their travels?

A: Some Japanese traveling overseas might spend an entire day selecting gifts for people back home. The Japanese obsession with souvenirs is famous throughout the world.

地」の「産物」という意味だと思っている人が多いかもしれない。

ところが、もとは「お土産」とは書かなかった。「宮笥」と書いたのである。宮笥とは、神札をはった板のこと。その昔、伊勢参りなど、村を代表してお宮参りをした人が、村人のために買って帰ったのが、この宮笥だった。

お宮参りといっても、村の外には、邪鬼悪霊がうようよいると考えられていた時代。村を代表してお参りする男性に、村人たちは、賽銭を渡して、自分の祈願を頼んだ。

これが餞別の風習の始まりだが、神社にたどりついた男は、その餞別で、村人のぶんの宮笥を買った。やがて、神社前で、土地の物産が売られるようになり、それらも、宮笥にならって「みやげ」と呼ばれるようになったのである。

もともと、お土産は、宮笥に便乗して土地の産物を売りはじめたものである。

Q: 日本独特の家紋は、なぜできたのか？

A: ──────── どの家にも、その家ごとに決まった「家紋」がある。しかし、最近の日常生活では、家紋が重要な意味をもつ機会が少なくなり、自分の家の

The Japanese word for these gifts, *o-miyage*, is written with characters that make many people think the word's etymology is "local product." However, the word was not originally written in that way. The original meaning of *miyage* was "shrine board." When people went to Ise Shrine or other sacred spots as representatives of their villages, they would buy small pieces of wood called *miyage* to bring back for their neighbors.

In those days, people thought even when they were just visiting a shrine that the world outside their village was lurking with evil spirits and demons. So the village representatives would be given offerings by other villagers and asked to pray on their behalf.

This was the start of the custom of giving gifts to people leaving on journeys. When the representatives reached the shrines, they would use that money to buy *miyage* boards for their neighbors. Later, local products came to be sold near the shrines, and those products came to be called *miyage* as well.

Thus today's souvenirs started out with people who took advantage of the shrines' *miyage* board business to sell local products to travelers.

Q: Why did a unique style of family crest develop in Japan?

A: Every Japanese family has its own family crest. These days, though, family crests seldom have much significance in daily life, and increasing numbers of people don't even

家紋が何であるかを知らない人も増えている。紋付きの和服をつくるときや、「家紋をおつけいたします」という、五月人形などの宣伝文句に乗せられたとき、初めて家紋を意識することになるのが、現代の一般的日本人である。

さて、その家紋、平安初期に、公家たちが当時の乗用車だった牛車につけたのが、そのはじまりだ。いってみれば、現在のタクシーのマークのようなものだったのだ。

当時、公家たちが集まる宴には、牛車がズラリと並んだ。しかし、いずれも黒漆の塗られた牛車、どれが誰のものかわかりにくく、そこで黒漆の上に金蒔絵で印をつけた。ここから、家紋の歴史はスタートした。

その後、地紋と呼ばれる着物に織りだすものが生まれ、大名らが嫁ぐ娘にもたせる結婚調度品などにも、家紋が入れられるようになる。

家紋の最盛期であった江戸時代には、1万2000種類もの家紋が存在した。

植物にちなんだデザインがもっとも多く、ご存じ天皇家の菊の紋章は、それが薬草であり、魔除けに効くということから決められた。

また、神に仕える家では、柏の葉を家紋にしていることが多いが、柏の葉はお供え物の下に敷くものだから、縁起がいいというわけだ。植物以外では、星、月、波、水などの自然現象、舟や車輪、弓など人の用いる道具、あるいは漢数字を図案化したものがある。

know what their crest is. The Japanese today start thinking about their crests only when they have kimono marked with the crest or when they succumb to advertising for ceremonial dolls or other products that promise individualized insignia.

Japanese family crests got their start back in the early Heian period, when nobles in the imperial entourage began putting the marks on the cattle-drawn carriages they rode in. The crests were like the company logos seen now on taxis.

When the nobility gathered for a banquet, their carriages would be parked outside. Since every carriage was painted with black lacquer, it was hard to tell which was which, so sprinkled gold patterns were applied to the lacquer. That marked the start of the family crest tradition.

Later people began to have crests woven into their kimono, and crests were also put on dowry items for the daughters from noble families. The boom time for family crests was the Edo period, when some 12,000 different patterns existed.

The most common designs use plants motifs. The well-known chrysanthemum crest of the imperial household depicts a medicinal plant that was chosen because it was thought to drive away evil.

Families who operate shrines often have crests with oak leaf patterns. Oak leaves are thought to be lucky because they are placed under religious offerings.

Other designs include stars, the moon, waves, water and natural phenomena, boats, wheels, bows, artifacts, and Chinese numerals.

Q: 日本人は、なぜあんなに多くの年賀状を書くのか？

A: ──────── 年賀状を廃止したらどうかという意見がある。12月中に新年のあいさつを書き、元旦に読むのがわざとらしいというのが理由の1つのようだが、その年賀状が一般的になったのは、明治時代。むろん、近代的な郵便制度が日本に導入されたあとのことである。

新年のあいさつは古代、もしくは平安時代からあったという説があるが、江戸時代に武士や商人のあいだで、近隣には使者をだし、離れた人には、飛脚にたくして年賀のあいさつをする習慣があった。

やがて、武士や裕福な商人のあいだでは、年始のあいさつを書いた書状が届けられるようになる。これが年賀状のルーツといわれ、しだいに習慣となっていった。

さらに、この習慣は、明治6年（1873年）明治政府が郵便葉書を発売、料金の安い葉書を年賀のあいさつにつかうようになって急速に広がっていった。

12月中に投函された年賀葉書が、元旦から配達されるようになったのは明治39年（1906年）のことだが、これから、すでに90年以上が経つ。現在は、交通機関や電話の発達で、日ごろから、友人と連絡をとりあう機会は多いので、年賀状廃止論が出てくるのももっともかもしれない。

Q: Why do Japanese people send so many New Year's cards?

A: Some people have proposed doing away with the custom of sending New Year's cards. One reason is that it seems phony and insincere to send a bunch of greeting cards in December and then read the ones received on New Year's Day.

New Year's cards became popular in the Meiji period after Japan adopted a modern postal system.

According to some accounts, though, New Year's greetings date back to the Heian period or even earlier. During the Edo period, members of the warrior and merchant classes would convey greetings to each other at New Year's by dispatching servants to nearby neighbors and long-distance runners to those who lived far away.

Later the samurai and wealthy merchants began exchanging written greetings. That custom, the precursor of today's New Year's cards, gradually took root.

After the Meiji government started selling inexpensive postal cards in 1873, the number of people exchanging yearly greetings rapidly increased.

It was in 1906 that New Year's cards mailed in December began to be delivered on New Year's Day. In the more than ninety years since, transportation, telephones, and other means of communication have made it easier for people to keep in touch with friends. It's no wonder that someone has proposed doing away with New Year's cards altogether.

Q: 日本人は、なぜ箸を使うようになったのか？

A: ─────── もともと日本の箸の原型は、1本の棒だった。これを曲げ、和裁の糸きり鋏のようにして、食べ物を刺したり、はさんだりして箸はつかわれていた。"はし"という名も、両端を曲げてくっつけたことから生まれたといわれる。

　といっても、これは弥生時代末期の話で、もっぱら神事儀礼の場で使用され、ふだんの食事には用いられていなかった。

　さて、現在のような2本1組の箸がつかわれるようになったのは、8世紀、奈良時代のこと。それ以前、箸の普及に努めたのは、かの聖徳太子である。彼はすでに2本の箸をつかっていた中国からの使節団を迎えるにあたり、日本を「箸もつかえないような野蛮な国」と思われたくないために、使節団の歓迎会出席者全員に箸をつかう"特訓"をさせたという。

　この特訓が功を奏し、その当日は日本側も器用に箸をつかいこなしたが、残念ながら隋の使節団の見聞記『隋書倭国伝』には、「手をもってこれを食らう」と記されてしまっている。というのも、当時の一般庶民は、みんな手づかみで食事をしていたからだ。

　そのときは、聖徳太子の特訓も徒労に終わったようにみえたが、1世紀後には、庶民にも箸が普及したのだから、太子の努力も無駄ではなかったともいえる。ともかく、日本人がいまの

Q: Why do the Japanese use chopsticks?

A: Japanese chopsticks originated as a single rod of wood. The rod would be bent in the middle like a pair of traditional Japanese scissors and the ends were used to stab and grab food. In fact, the Japanese word for chopsticks, *hashi*, is said to come from a homophone meaning "end" or "tip," because it was the two ends of the rod that were bent and held together.

Those protochopsticks existed in the late Yayoi period, but they were used only for religious ceremonies, not for everyday meals.

The two-rod set that we know today as chopsticks was adopted widely in the eighth century, during the Nara period. Their use had been promoted earlier by the influential Prince Shōtoku. In those days, people in China already used two chopsticks, so before a Chinese delegation came to Japan the prince required all Japanese attending the welcoming reception to practice using them. His reason was that he didn't want the Chinese to think that Japan was a country of barbarians who couldn't even use chopsticks.

The training was successful, and the Japanese attending the banquet were able to use their chopsticks with skill. Unfortunately, the report prepared by the Chinese delegates—known as *Zuisho Wakokuden* in Japanese—stated that the Japanese ate with their hands. After all, that was how common people still ate.

It would seem that Prince Shōtoku's efforts had been wasted, but a century later even the common people were using chopsticks. The prince had not labored in vain. Thus Japanese now eat with chopsticks because Prince Shōtoku

ような2本の箸をつかうようになったのは、聖
徳太子の大国に対する見栄のためともいえるの
である。

Q: 日本人は、なぜおじぎをするようになったのか？

A: ──────── 日本人がおじぎをしはじめたのは、大化の改新
（645年）のころからだと言われる。

それまで、日本では目上の人に対して土下座
をしていた。邪馬台国について記した『魏志倭
人伝』にも、「下戸（庶民）が、大人（貴族）
と話すときは、うずくまってひざまずき、両手
を地について敬意をあらわす」と書かれている。

それが、大化の改新の際、土下座をやめ、お
じぎに変更したのである。

おじぎは中国の立礼をまねたものだったが、
おじぎをすると、視線をはずして、頭を下げて
無防備な姿勢を取る。それによって、攻撃の意
図をもっていないことを示していた。

現在の剣道では、おじぎのあと "打ち合い"
をするが、本来、おじぎは相手に対して敵意が
なく、服従することを伝える意味があったので
ある。

ただし、大化の改新当時、おじぎはなかなか
広まらなかった。682年、そこで天武天皇が、
急遽「いまでも、昔ながらのひざまずくもの
（跪礼）や、腹ばってするおじぎ（匍匐礼）が

wanted to show off to the neighboring superpower.

Q: Why do the Japanese bow when greeting each other?

A: The Japanese are said to have taken up bowing around the time of the Taika Reform in 645.

Before then, people meeting their superiors would kneel on the ground. According to the third-century Chinese account of Japan, which is called *Gishi Wajinden* in Japanese (this work is also known for its intriguing description of the kingdom of Yamatai), "When the common people speak to nobles, they show their respect by kneeling on the ground and placing both hands on the ground."

When the Taika Reform was implemented, kneeling was replaced by bowing, in imitation of the similar practice in China.

A bowing person lowers his gaze and drops his head in a posture of defenselessness. This shows that the person has no intention of attacking.

In the martial art of *kendō*, competitors bow before they fight. Originally, though, bowing was supposed to show submission and a lack of hostility toward the other person.

The custom of bowing did not become widespread after the Taika Reform, so in 682 Emperor Tenmu issued an urgent proclamation: "People continue to bow in the old styles of kneeling or lying face down. From now on,

行われている。これからは、古い形式のおじぎ
をすべてやめ、『立礼』に統一せよ」と命令し
ている。

天皇の号令一下、おじぎは、日本人のあいだ
に広まっていったのである。

Q: 日本では、なぜ目下の者から紹介するのか？

A: ──────── 日本で人を紹介するとき、目下の者から紹介す
る。そして、目下の者が先におじぎをし、それ
から目上の人が「こんにちは」とおじぎを返す。

ところが欧米では、反対なのである。目上の
人を先に紹介し、目上の人から先に握手を求め
るのが、ふつうである。

日本では、目下から紹介する習慣は、古来の
「取り次ぎの作法」が受け継がれたものといわ
れている。「取り次ぎの作法」とは、来客があ
ると、門番から玄関番へ取り次ぎ、玄関番から
家の執事に、そして執事から側近へ取り次ぎ、
最後に主人へ取り次ぐという習慣のことであ
る。

この、目下の者から順に取り次いでいくとい
うルールが、家の外でも広がり、目下の者から
あいさつする習慣になったと考えられるのであ
る。

ちなみに、日本に、この「取り次ぎの作法」
が生まれたのは、家の構造に理由があった。昔
の屋敷は、門から入ると玄関があり、さらに事

these old-fashioned methods must be abandoned. Bow standing up!"

That imperial edict is what made bowing so popular in Japan.

Q: Why are lower-ranked people introduced first in Japan?

A: When a group of people is introduced to someone in Japan, the introductions proceed from those lower on the totem pole to those nearer the top. The lower-ranked people bow first, followed by the higher-ranked, who bow and exchange greetings.

In the West, though, the order is reversed. The top-ranked person is the first to be introduced and to shake hands.

The Japanese custom of starting at the bottom is said to derive from the old etiquette used for receiving visitors to a wealthy person's residence. When a visitor arrived, he would be handed over from the gatekeeper to the doorman, from the doorman to the butler, from the butler to the master's personal servant, and finally to the master himself.

That practice of starting at the bottom and working one's way up is thought to have been adopted outside the home as well, so the lower-ranked people became the first to greet the other party.

The visitor etiquette came about because of the way large Japanese homes were designed. In the old days, a visitor would first pass through the gate before coming to the

務をつかさどる者の部屋があって、そのずっと奥に部屋があった。奥にいくほど身分の高い者がいたことから、こんな習慣が生まれたのである。

Q: 日本では、なぜ火葬が多いのか？

A: ―――― 火で燃やして灰にしたり、そのまま土に埋めたり、ミイラにしたり、水に流したりと、死者を葬る方法は、民族や国によってさまざまである。

なかでも、私たち日本人にとってビックリなのが、中国チベット自治区やインドの一部などで行われている鳥葬だ。遺体を山へ運び、ハゲワシについばませるというものだ。

ただ、これも、遺体をポンと山に遺棄するだけではない。日本の葬式と同様、昔からの細かなしきたりがあり、遺体処理人は山頂にある決められた場所に遺体を運び、遺体の背中や胸、腹を刃物で切り刻む。脳も食べやすいように石で頭を砕く。

処理人が立ち去ると、それを見計らったようにハゲワシが飛んでくる。遺体は1時間もたたないうちに跡形もなくなるといい、見るかぎりでは残酷なやり方だ。だが、チベットでは、空が宇宙生成の五元素の1つ。鳥が死者の魂を空中に運んでくれるのだと考えられていて、そのための鳥葬なのである。

front door. Inside the door would be the rooms of those who handled household matters, and further inside were the rooms where the owners lived. The farther you went inside, the higher the ranks of the people. And that's how these customs originated.

Q: Why is cremation so common in Japan?

A: Burning to ashes, burying underground, making into mummies, setting adrift in water—these are the different methods used by the peoples and countries of the world to dispose of the dead.

One method that surprises Japanese people is the sky burial used in Tibet and some parts of India. The corpse is taken to the mountains and allowed to be consumed by vultures.

The body is not just abandoned. Just as at Japanese funerals, there are detailed procedures that have been followed for generations. The people handling the body first take it to a specified place on a mountaintop. There they use knives to cut openings in the back, chest, and stomach. They even break the skull with rocks—all to make the body easier to eat.

As soon as the workers leave the body, vultures come swooping down as if they had been waiting. In less than an hour the corpse is gone without a trace. This may seem like a cruel method, but in Tibet the sky is regarded as one of the five elements of the universe. The Tibetans believe that the birds carry the dead person's soul into the sky. In fact, that's the purpose of the sky burial.

ところで日本では、地方にわずかに土葬が残っているものの、97パーセントが火葬になっている。これは仏教の影響で、釈迦は死んだときに、ガンジス川の川原で火葬されたといわれている。

　仏教が日本に伝わってくると、火葬で死者の肉体を消滅させることは、より魂が浄化されることであり、中途半端に肉体が残っていると未練が残って極楽浄土で安楽できないと解釈された。

　しかしそれでも、火葬が一般化するのは明治以降のことで、遺体に埋葬面積や衛生管理の問題から、都市部に土葬禁止令が出たのがきっかけだった。

　「復活のためには肉体が必要」という理由で火葬を禁じていたキリスト教でも、明治時代の日本と同じような理由で、いまでは火葬を認めている。

Q: 日本人は昔、なぜちょんまげを結うようになったのか？

A: ─────ちょんまげ──いうまでもなく、時代劇でおなじみのヘアスタイル。額から頭のてっぺんまで剃りあげ、残った髪を後方に結びあげる。世界にも類をみない独特の髪型だ。しかし、あのユニークな髪型も、最初は、ごく実用的な理由から生まれたという。

　話は、平安時代の末期にさかのぼる。この時代、新しい"職種"が生まれた。武士だ。

　武士は、戦うのが仕事だから、鎧をつけ、兜

In Japan, 97 percent of the dead are cremated. Intact burial remains in only a few areas. The preference for cremation comes from Buddhism, for Buddha is said to have been cremated on the banks of the River Ganges when he died.

After Buddhism was brought to Japan, it was believed that engulfing the dead person's flesh in flames would enable better purification of the person's soul. If some flesh remained, it was thought, the soul would still long for its existence on earth and would feel uneasy in heaven.

Nevertheless, it was only in the Meiji period that cremation became common in Japan; the reasons were a ban on burials in urban areas because of the lack of space and concerns about hygiene.

For Christians, cremation used to be banned because it was believed that the flesh was necessary for resurrection. Now, though, cremation is permitted, and the reasons are the same as in Meiji Japan.

Q: Why did the Japanese use to wear their hair in topknots?

A: The topknot, called *chonmage* in Japanese, is the men's hairstyle seen in samurai epics and other historical dramas. The top of the head is shaved from the forehead to the crown, and the remaining hair is gathered into a knot on the top of the head. Although *chonmage* is unlike any other hairstyle in the world, it was created for practical reasons.

The time was the late Heian period. A new job classification had been created: the samurai.

The samurai's job was to fight, so he wore armor and

をかぶる。さて、問題はこの兜だった。髪を伸ばした頭に兜をかぶると、頭がむれて仕方がない。そこで、兜のてっぺんに穴をあけ、その真下にあたる頭頂部を剃りあげたのだ。これが、ちょんまげの原型だ。

　さて、なぜ、その兜用の特殊な髪型が、日本全体に広がっていったか。

　これは、当時の庶民にかっこいいと受けとめられたから。武士のスタイルということで、勇ましく見え、勇気のシンボルになったわけだ。

　室町・戦国時代には、庶民や農民もほとんどが髪を剃るようになり、しだいに形が工夫され、てっぺんだけでなく、額まで剃るようになって、ちょんまげの形ができあがった。

　明治になって消えるまで、ざっと800年、日本男性の主流のヘアスタイルだったわけだ。七三の横分けなんて、ちょんまげの歴史と比べるとまだまだ全然かなわない。

donned a helmet. But that helmet posed a problem. If the warrior wore his hair long, he would get terribly hot and sweaty inside the helmet. Therefore an opening was made on the top of helmets, and samurai shaved the crowns of their heads under the hole. That was the origin of the topknot.

But that raises another question: Why did this hairstyle for helmet-wearers come to be worn by men throughout Japan?

It was because the commoner thought it was neat. It was the style of the samurai. It looked tough and brave.

In the Muromachi and Warring States periods, almost all peasants and common people shaved the tops of their heads. Eventually they started shaving their foreheads as well, and the *chonmage* style took shape.

For eight hundred years, until it died out in the Meiji period, the topknot was the main hairstyle for Japanese men. Compared to its long history, the standard side-parted hairstyle worn by today's white-collar workers is a distant runner-up.

日本人の「こだわり」の雑学

Q: なぜ、日本人は自分専用の食器にこだわるのか？

A: ──────お茶碗やお箸は、家族それぞれに決まっているという家庭が多いはず。お父さんのお茶碗が大きめで、お母さんのが小ぶりだったりするのだが、年齢の近い兄弟では、同じ大きさの茶碗でも、絵柄で、誰のものと決めていたりする。

　自分の専用の食器にこだわるのは、一つには昔、米などの穀物を神聖なものと考えていたことの名残だといわれる。もともと、お米を食べるとき、掌にのせて食べていた。自分の掌にのせることで、神に感謝しながら食べたのである。

　やがて、掌は葉っぱになり、食器になっていったが、豊作を神に感謝する気持ちは受け継がれた。そのため、自分専用の器にのせ、唾液が他人と混じらないようにしたのである。

　平城京跡から発掘された土器には、すでに、裏面に名前を書き、所有者をはっきりさせているものもある。

　また、自分専用の食器が、ご飯を食べるお茶

CHAPTER 6
Trivia on Japanese Tastes

Q: Why do the Japanese like having their own rice bowls?

A: In many Japanese families, each person has his or her own rice bowl and chopsticks. The father's rice bowl may be a bit larger and the mother's a bit smaller. Even if brothers close in age have bowls the same size, the bowls can be distinguished by the different patterns.

One reason for this insistence on having individual dinnerware is that long ago rice and other grains were regarded as sacred objects. When people ate rice, they placed it in the palms of their hands as a sign of thanks to the gods.

Later the hands were replaced by leaves and then by bowls, but the feeling of gratitude to the gods for a bountiful harvest remained. People would put the rice in their individual bowls so that their saliva would not become mixed with another person's saliva.

Some earthenware vessels found in the ruins of the eighth-century Heijōkyō city in Nara have names written on their bottoms to identify their owners.

The use of individualized utensils, though, was limited

碗にかぎられるのも、主食が特別だったことを示している。カレーライスの皿やラーメンのどんぶりはもちろん、みそ汁のお椀でも、自分専用のものをもつ人は少ないはずである。

Q: 日本人はなぜ、こんなにも風呂好きなのか？

A: —————外国人には、シャワーだけで平気という人が多いが、日本人はそうはいかない。海外を長く貧乏旅行をしていると、お風呂が無性に恋しくなるようだ。シャワーだけの生活には、がまんできなくなってくるのだ。

　日本人が風呂を好きなのは、一つは日本独特の気候のせいといわれている。夏は高温多湿で、冬は寒い。熱いお風呂につかることで、暑さと寒さを吹き飛ばすことができるからである。

　しかし、それ以上にお湯につかることで、心がリラックスできるのも風呂好きの理由だろう。建て前社会といわれる日本では、家の外で気を張っている人が多い。

　「男子家を出ずれば7人の敵あり」といわれる国。外へ出ると、知らず知らず心と体を緊張させているのである。

　だから家に帰って裸になると一気にリラックスする。「食事にしますか？　お風呂にしますか？」と問われ、「風呂から」というお父さんが多いのも、まずお風呂で心と体の緊張を解きたいからである。

　お風呂でする裸のつきあい。昔から、銭湯は

to rice bowls, because this staple was given special status. Today, few people insist on having their own bowls for curry, *ramen*, or *miso* soup.

Q: Why do Japanese like taking baths so much?

A: Many foreigners don't mind taking only showers, but showers alone won't do for the Japanese. Japanese travelers on low-budget overseas trips start to miss baths desperately. They can't stand to have only showers.

One reason Japanese like baths is the climate of Japan. Summers are hot and humid, and winters are cold. A hot bath provides escape from both extremes.

But an even more important reason why people like hot baths is that it allows them to relax. In Japan, where one's public persona is all-important, many people feel stressed out when they are away from home. In fact, a Japanese proverb states: "When a man leaves his home, he faces seven enemies." Outside the home, both body and soul become tense.

So returning home and taking off one's clothes provides immediate relaxation. When asked by their wives whether they want to eat dinner or take a bath when they come home from work, many men choose the bath first, for bathing provides both physical and spiritual release.

Baths—public baths in particular—give people the chance

建て前社会に生きる日本人が、本音を語る数少ない場所だった。

Q: 日本人は、なぜ"血液型"の話が好きなのか？

A: ──── 合コンでの話題に血液型から入る学生は多い。「ねえ、何型？」という会話から、初対面同士でもけっこう話が盛り上がるのだ。さりげなく、「O型の女性とB型の男って、相性いいんだよね」といえば、親近感も増す。口説きの導入部にもなるのだが、これほど血液型の話題が好きな国民というのも珍しい。

冷静に考えれば、話している本人たちも遊び感覚。たった4つしかない血液型で、性格を分類できると、かならずしも信じきっているわけではなさそうだ。

それでも、気に食わない人がいると、「あの人はA型だから、私の苦手なタイプ」と妙に納得したりする。他人との相性や関係を気にしすぎて、その理由づけに血液型を利用しているのである。

「O型の女性とB型の男って、相性いいんだよね」というのも、根拠がないのに、連帯感をもつことで安心しているにすぎないのではなかろうか。つまり、血液型占いを信じるというより、自分や他人を一定の枠組みでとらえて安心しているのである。

to bare both their bodies and their souls. For centuries, the public bath has been one of the few places where appearance-obsessed Japanese have been able to express their real feelings.

Q: Why do the Japanese like to talk about their blood types?

A: At student parties, the conversation often begins with talk about blood types.

"Hey, what's your blood type?"

That question works well to break the ice among people who have just met. If someone mentions casually that, "Type O women are really compatible with Type B men," then the people involved feel closer. (It also works as a pick-up line.) Few people like to talk about blood types as much as the Japanese do.

However, people who talk about blood types usually aren't being serious. Most don't believe that it is really possible to classify personalities into only four categories.

Still, if there's somebody you don't like, it's often easy to get others to understand your feelings by saying, "That guy has Type A blood. I don't get along with people like that." Blood types provide a convenient excuse for people obsessed with compatibility and relations with others.

Even though there's no basis for claims like "Type O women are really compatible with Type B men," such statements create bonds that make people feel more comfortable. Rather than believing in blood-type fortunetelling, people feel relieved at being able to put themselves and others into neat pigeonholes.

これも、血液型のように他愛ないもので人をグループ分けできるほど、日本人同士がよく似ていることの裏返しといえる。人種や民族、生活様式の違う人たちが入り交じった国では、人々を単純に類型分けできない。

ましてや、4つの血液型で性格を分けることなど不可能に近いことである。日本人はお互い似すぎていて、差別化しにくいからこそ、血液型というフィクションで区別して、自分のアイデンティティを保とうとしているといえるのかもしれない。

ほとんどの国で、血液型は輸血のためだけに利用され、性格を語る材料にされることはほとんどない。

Q: 日本人は、なぜ相手の「年齢」にこだわるのか？

A: ──── 日本を旅したフランス人が、「何回も年齢を聞かれるから、いっぺんに100歳も年を取った気がする」とぼやいていた。たしかに、外国では、ふつうの会話で、いきなり相手の年齢を聞くことはない。相手が何歳だろうと気にならないからである。

ところが、日本には相手の年齢がわからないと落ち着かない人が多い。年功序列が徹底しているから、どう接していいのかわからなくなるのだ。

たとえば、名前の呼び方一つをとっても、相手が上なら「○○さん」となる。しかし、年下なら「○○くん」と呼んだり、呼び捨てにしてもいい。

That the Japanese are able to classify each other by a characteristic as foolish as blood type shows that the Japanese are very similar to each other. In a country that included people of many races, ethnic groups, and lifestyles, such simplistic grouping would be inconceivable.

In fact, it is practically impossible to classify people's personalities according to four blood types. Perhaps the reason this blood-type fantasy has been created is that, since the Japanese are so similar to each other and difficult to tell apart, blood types help people maintain a sense of individual identity.

In other countries, blood types are thought about only for blood transfusions. Rarely are they ever discussed in relation to people's personalities.

Q: Why do the Japanese pay so much attention to people's ages?

A: A Frenchman visiting Japan once complained, "I've been asked my age so many times that I feel a century older." In other countries people normally do not ask how old a person is in day-to-day conversation. They don't really care about other people's ages.

In Japan, though, many people feel uncomfortable not knowing the age of someone they're talking to. They don't know how to deal with the other person, because age-based ranking is fundamental to Japanese society.

Even the forms of spoken address change. A man speaking to someone older will add the suffix *san* to the person's surname; to a younger person, he will use the more informal *kun* or omit the suffix entirely.

そのため、相手の年齢がわからないと、どう呼んでいいか迷ってしまう人さえいるのである。

　　また、この日本ではまったく関係のないところで、年齢を聞かれることもある。たとえば、ビジネスホテルの宿泊名簿に、年齢欄や生年月日を書くところがある。

　　ある外国人が、「日本のホテルは生年月日占いで、部屋割りを決めるのか？」と不思議がっていたが、宿泊に年齢は関係ないはず。

　　外国ではまず聞かれないし、国によっては「年齢で部屋や扱いを差別した」と訴えられることすらありえる。

Q: 日本人は、なぜ大の大人でも電車のなかでマンガを読むのか？

A: ──────外国では、マンガ雑誌といえば、ほとんどが子供むけかスケベな大人むけ。だから、日本人の大人が、電車のなかでマンガを読むことが、外国人には理解できないらしい。

　　しかし、マンガの中身を読んでもらえば、外国人にも納得してもらえるはず。日本のマンガは、まず内容的にレベルが高く、大人が読むに堪えられる。マンガを読むから幼稚という決めつけは、日本では通用しない。

　　しかも、面白いマンガ雑誌が、週に何冊も発売される。毎週、続きを読もうとすると、電車のなかででも読まないと追いつかないという理由もあるのだろう。

　　さらにマンガは読めるスピードが速いから、

That's why some people get upset if they don't know the other person's age since they won't know how to talk to him.

In Japan, you might be asked your age at places where it doesn't matter at all. For example, the registration forms at business hotels ask visitors to write their age and birth date.

One foreigner wondered, "What, do Japanese hotels assign rooms based on horoscopes?" After all, age should not matter for lodging.

Outside Japan, hotels don't ask your age. In some countries hotels might even be sued for discrimination for providing rooms or services based on age.

Q: Why do Japanese adults read comic books on trains?

A: In other countries, almost all comic books are either for children or for adults who like pornography. That's why foreigners don't understand why Japanese adults read comics on trains.

If those foreigners were to read Japanese comics, though, they would understand. Comics in Japan are written in such a sophisticated way that even adults can enjoy them. In Japan, no one thinks that reading comics is a sign of childishness.

People read comics on trains because so many different magazines with interesting comics are published each week. If they want to keep up with the serials, they have no choice but to read them while commuting.

Comics are quick reads; many pages can be read

1区間の距離でもけっこう読みすすむことができる。だから、電車移動のあいだの短い時間には、活字ばかりの本より、マンガのほうがピッタリなのである。

また、反対に通勤時間が長いから、マンガを読む人も多い。1時間以上かかる電車のなかで、行きは新聞を読むが、帰りはマンガという人たちである。仕事疲れの体には、マンガのほうが気軽に読めるからだ。

外国人の目にどう映ろうと、日本人は、もはやマンガなしでは生きられない体になっている。

Q: 日本人は、なぜ好んで接待ゴルフをするのか？

A: ─────── 日曜の朝も早くから、接待ゴルフに出かけるお父さん。日本のビジネスに接待ゴルフは欠かせないが、こんな国はほかにない。もし外国で見かけたら、それはかならず日系企業がからんでいるはずだ。

日本でだけ接待ゴルフが盛んになったのは、一つには相手を舞い上がらせておいて、口説き落とすという日本流ビジネスの舞台になるからである。

接待ゴルフをよく知らない人は、ゴルフをしながら、ビジネスの交渉をすると思っているかもしれない。

しかし、プレー中、ビジネスの話はタブー。接待するほうは、相手に、いかに楽しくプレーしてもらうかに気を配っている。そのため、

between stations. That makes them better than text-only books for short train rides.

However, many people with long commutes also read comics. If they have to ride an hour or more to work each way, they'll often read a newspaper going to work and comic books on the way home. After a hard day's work, comics are easier to read.

So it doesn't matter what foreigners may think. Japanese people cannot live without comics.

Q: Why do the Japanese like playing golf with their business associates?

A: It's commonplace for Japanese businessmen to play golf with business associates, even early on Sunday mornings. Golf is an essential part of doing business in Japan. Not so in other countries. In fact, if you see businessmen playing golf elsewhere, they are almost certainly connected to a Japanese company.

One reason business golf has become popular only in Japan is that it provides a good setting for Japanese-style business, that is, kissing up to the other person in order to win him over.

People who aren't familiar with business golf may think that the players are talking business as they play. Actually, though, discussing business is verboten during the game. The person paying for the game tries hard to make his guest have a good time while playing. It's essential to complement the guest on his shots and thoroughly butter him up.

「ナイスショット！」の声をかけるなど、ひたすらおだてることが大切なのだ。

また、接待ゴルフで肝心なのは、相手が下手でも、負けてあげること。相手を勝たせて表彰し、高価な商品を手渡す。さらに、酒を飲ませ、相手をもちあげるだけもちあげておいたうえで、初めて、ビジネスの話をする。

つまり、相手に断れない状況をつくっておいて、固い防御を突破する。そのためにつかわれる舞台なのである。

ただし、心臓の弱い役員クラスが、コースに出る前、景気づけにビールを飲んでスタートしたところ、むずかしいショットに血圧がはねあがり、発作を起こして亡くなるというケースが、毎年200人はいる。

Q: 日本人は、なぜ団体旅行が好きなのか？

A: ──────── 世界広しといえども、団体旅行がいちばん好きなのは、日本人だろう。もちろん、外国への旅行に団体でいく国は多い。しかし、そんな場合も、2〜3人のグループが旅行会社のツアーに応募。手間や料金を節約するため、知らない者同士がいっしょに旅行するというケースが多い。

ところが、日本人は、会社や親睦会のメンバーが、丸ごと団体旅行する。

しかも、国内でも団体旅行するから、日本人の団体旅行好きは筋金入りである。

そうなったのも、少し前まで旅行といえば、小学校の遠足や修学旅行が中心だったからだろ

It's also important to lose. Even if your guest is a total duffer, you have to let him win, praise him loudly, and give him expensive prizes. Only later, after you have had a few drinks and lifted his spirits as much as possible, do you start talking business.

In other words, the secret is to break through the other person's defenses and create a situation where he can't say no. That's the purpose of golf.

Sometimes older top executives with weak hearts will have a few beers to pick up their spirits before going out on the golf course. When they are faced with a difficult shot, their blood pressure shoots up, they have a seizure, and some die. That happens about 200 times a year.

Q: Why do Japanese people like traveling in tour groups?

A: Throughout the world, nobody likes traveling in tour groups as much as the Japanese. Of course, people in many other countries also travel abroad in groups. In those cases, though, they usually sign up in parties of two or three with an agency and travel with strangers. For them, a tour group is just a way to save money and bother.

Japanese often travel in big groups of people from the same company or social organization. And they travel in groups even within Japan. The Japanese love for tours is most enduring.

The reason is that until recently travel for the Japanese meant excursions or trips with school groups. Nowadays

う。いまでこそ、家族で海外旅行する人も多い。しかし、20年ほど前まで、「旅行にいくぞ」といえば、学校の修学旅行や臨海学校、林間学校が主だった。

　40歳以上にとって、旅行といえば学校や会社での団体旅行。つい、いまでも団体旅行を選んでしまうのである。担任の先生に引率されるように、添乗員の後をついていくことが楽しいのである。

　外国で、男性ばかり20人以上の団体旅行客といえば、95パーセントの確率で日本人である。そしてあとの5パーセントは、韓国人である。

Q: 日本人は、スポーツの中でもなぜ野球がとくに好きなのか？

A: ──────野球は、国際的にいえば、かなりマイナーなスポーツ。アメリカ、中南米と極東で、ほそぼそと行われているにすぎない。それなのに、日本の男性には、野球をした経験のない人というのは、まずいない。はっきりとはいえないが、たぶん日本人は世界でもっとも野球が好きな国民の1つだろう。

　日本人は、なぜこんなに野球が好きなのだろうか？　それは、野球のルールが、日本人の嗜好というか好みにぴったりだったからと分析されている。

　具体的にいうと、第一には、ルール上、役割分担がはっきりしていることだ。投手が投げ、打者が打つ。打者にも、1番から9番まで、そ

many people travel overseas with their families, but until about twenty years ago most travel was with school groups or to camps at the sea or in the mountains.

For people over forty years of age, travel is synonymous with a tour with a company or school group, so they still choose to go in groups. Just as they used to tag along behind their teachers, now they enjoy following the tour leader.

If you're outside Japan and you see a tour group of twenty or more men, there's a 95 percent chance that they're Japanese. The other 5 percent chance is that they're Korean.

Q: Why do the Japanese like baseball so much?

A: Internationally, baseball is a minor sport. It's played only in the United States, Latin America, and the Far East. Despite its lowly status, it'd be difficult to find a Japanese man who has never played baseball. It's hard to be certain, but it seems likely that the Japanese are some of the biggest baseball fans in the world.

What makes the Japanese like baseball so much? One analysis says that it's because the rules of baseball provide what the Japanese like.

For one thing, the rules call for a clear allocation of responsibilities. The pitchers pitch; the hitters hit. The batters are numbered from one to nine, and each has his own

れぞれの役割がある。そのあたりが、日本人の集団主義、組織好きに、ぴったりなのだ。

その役割分担のなか、両チームの監督がさまざまに用兵の妙を競い合う点も、日本人好みといえる。日本人は、単に力が強いものが勝つという単純明快なスポーツよりも、そこに作戦性が加味されることで、さらに強い興味を覚える。

「ここはバントだよ」「いや、打っていかなくちゃ」という駆け引きがあってこそ、醍醐味を覚えるのだ。

また、野球というスポーツには、そういう駆け引きを十分に味わえるゆったりとした間がある。

プロ野球では、しばしば試合の長さが問題になるが、もし野球が1時間で終わるスポーツなら、ここまで人気が長続きしてこなかったに違いない。

さて、スピーディーなスポーツの代表であり、世界的なメジャースポーツであるサッカー。日本でも、野球の人気をこえる日はくるのだろうか。

Q: 日本人は、なぜ車をいつもピカピカに磨きあげるのか？

A: ──────── 日本人には、なぜかクルマを磨きあげることが快感という人が多い。

ホコリだらけの汚いクルマが当たり前の他国では、考えられないような光景だが、それだけ日本人はきれい好きで、潔癖性の人が多いのだろう。

愛車をピカピカに磨きあげる人には、クルマ

role to play. The game is ideal for the Japanese love of groups and organizations.

Japanese also like the role played by the coaches, who compete by the use of subtle tactics. They are more interested in sports that involve strategy than in simple, easy-to-understand competitions in which the stronger side wins.

What makes baseball fun is the chance for the fans to get involved in the strategy: "Now he's going to bunt." "No, he's got to swing at it."

And there's enough time in baseball for spectators to enjoy that strategy.

While people often complain about the length of baseball games, baseball never would have remained as popular if the games lasted only an hour.

The perfect example of a fast sport is soccer, the biggest sport in the world. Do you think soccer will ever become more popular than baseball in Japan?

Q: Why do the Japanese keep their cars sparkling clean?

A: For some reason, many Japanese enjoy washing and polishing their cars. That would be hard to imagine in countries where dirty cars are the norm. It just shows again how obsessed the Japanese are with cleanliness.

Many people who keep their vehicles spotless think of

を自分の部屋のように思っている人も多い。住宅事情の悪い日本では、クルマのなかだけが1人になれたり、好きな音楽が聴ける場所という人もいる。いってみれば、"書斎"のようなものだから、ピカピカに磨きたくなるわけだ。

　そんな人のクルマに乗せてもらうと、車内をぬいぐるみやアクセサリーで飾ったり、ジュウタンをしいて土足厳禁にしていたりしていて驚かされることがある。

Q: 日本人は、なぜバッジが好きなのか？

A: ──────日本のサラリーマンは、スーツの襟に会社のバッジをつけている。入館証代わりという意味もあるが、プライベートのときにもつけたがる人は多い。

　一般の人がそのバッジを見ても、どこの会社かわからないが、一流企業の人ほどつけたがることを考えると、どうも誇示したがっているらしい。

　しかし、欧米では、襟に会社のバッジをつける習慣はない。会社への帰属意識に乏しいので、自分の会社を他人に知らせる必要はないのである。

　それに対して、日本人は、集団・組織への帰属意識が強い。他人に、所属の組織を知らせないと不安になるほどで、日本人は、個人ではなく、組織に帰属することでプライドを保とうとする。

their cars as their home. Because of the cramped living conditions in Japan, often the automobile is the only place where people can be alone and listen to their favorite music. The car is like a den, and that's why people try to keep their vehicles sparkling clean.

If you ever ride in one of those pampered cars, you may be surprised at the stuffed animals and other decorations inside. Some drivers even put carpets on the floor and make passengers take off their shoes before getting in.

Q: Why do Japanese employees like to wear lapel pins?

A: Many Japanese salarymen wear pins on the lapels of their suits with the logo of their employer. While one purpose is to identify the wearer as an employee when he enters company premises, many men sport the pins even when they aren't working.

Most people can't identify a company just by looking at the lapel pin, but the wearers seem to feel pride in wearing it, for it is the employees of leading companies that like to wear them most.

In Europe and America, there is no similar custom of wearing company lapel pins. People there feel little sense of loyalty to their companies, so there's no need to let other people know where they work.

The Japanese, though, have a strong sense of belonging to groups and organizations. In fact, many take such pride in their official affiliations—rather than in themselves as individuals—that they feel uneasy if they don't let others know which group they belong to.

だから、プライベートでも、襟のバッジをはず
そうとしない。そのくせ、会社が不祥事をおこ
すと、カッコ悪いだのといってはずす人が多い。
　欧米の企業では珍しく、イタリアのフェラー
リは、有名な「跳ね馬」のバッジをつけること
で知られている。ただし彼らは、その会社の伝
統を誇りにおもっているのであって、フェラー
リに所属する自分を誇っているわけではないよ
うだ。

Q: 日本人は、なぜ「紅白」戦にこだわるのか？

A: ──────── 日本では『紅白歌合戦』だが、韓国では、『青
　　　　　　　白歌合戦』。2チームを色で分ける対抗戦は世
　　　　　　　界でも珍しく、日本と韓国くらいである。

　ちなみに、韓国の「青白」は、青竜・白虎に
ちなんでというが、日本の「紅白」のルーツは、
源平の戦いにあるという。
　当時、源氏の白旗に対して、平家は赤旗を掲
げて戦った。

　これを真似て、明治19年（1886年）、一高
対高商のボートレースで、応援団がそれぞれ赤
と白の旗をもって応援したと記録にある。翌
日、新聞が「まるで壇ノ浦の源平合戦のようだ
った」と報じたが、この応援風景がきっかけで、
以来、紅白対抗戦が行われるようになったとい
う。

So Japanese salarymen don't take off their badges even after working hours. Only if their company gets involved in a scandal do many remove the pins out of shame.

Rare among Western companies is the Italian firm Ferrari, whose employees wear pins with the famous jumping-horse logo. However, Ferrari workers wear the badge because they are proud of the company's traditions, not because they are proud of themselves for working there.

Q: Why do the Japanese like contests between red and white teams?

A: Japan's popular New Year's Eve televised song contest is called "*Kōhaku Uta Gassen*," literally, "The Song Battle Between Red and White." In Korea, a similar program is "The Song Battle Between Blue and White." Few countries besides Japan and Korea divide competing teams by color.

The Korean blue and white come from the traditional colors of the dragon and tiger that represent East and West. The roots of Japan's red and white date back to the twelfth-century struggle between the Taira and Minamoto families. The Taira forces fought under a red flag and the Minamoto under a white.

At a college boat race in 1886, red and white were worn by the respective supporters of the schools that later became Tokyo and Hitotsubashi Universities. The next day, a newspaper reported that "it looked just like the Battle of Dannoura between the Taira and Minamoto." That boat race started the tradition of red–white contests.

源平のうちでも、先に旗を掲げたのは、源氏の白旗。文字も書ける一般的な旗で、白旗自体に意味はなかったと考えられている。

　その白旗に対抗して、平家は赤旗を掲げるようになったが、赤旗を選んだのには、深い意味がある。

　当時、宮中では、その位によって身に着けてもいい色が決められていた。天皇は絹の白、皇太子は黄丹（赤みを帯びた黄色）などだが、赤は、貴族のなかでもきわめて高い位しか身に着けることを許されていなかった。

　つまり、平家の赤旗は、源氏の白旗に対抗するとともに、平家の強い貴族志向を表していたのである。

　私たちが、何気なく目にする紅白対抗戦の裏には、源平の対抗意識の血が流れているのである。

Q: 日本人は、なぜ屋台が好きなのか？

A: ──────屋台のラーメン屋には、若い女性客もけっこう多い。オヤジが幅をきかせている店にいくことを嫌がる高校生や学生でも、屋台なら許せるという。オジサンから若い人まで、屋台が人気を集めるルーツをたどっていくと、武士の時代の心得につきあたるとの説がある。

　戦国時代、武士の心得に「早飯、早糞、早支度」というのがあった。武士は、いつでも戦闘の準備ができていないといけない。

In the Taira–Minamoto conflict, it was the Minamoto side that first used a flag. Plain white banners were chosen so that characters could be written on them. The color white is not thought to have had any meaning.

In contrast to the white flag, the Minamoto forces started using a red flag. The choice of red had a more profound significance.

At that time, people at the imperial court were only allowed to wear certain colors depending on their rank. The emperor wore white silk, the crown prince a reddish yellow. Only the highest nobles were allowed to wear red.

Thus the red of the Taira flag not only represented their opposition to Minamoto, it also showed their drive to strengthen their position among the court nobility.

Behind today's casual use of red and white in Japanese contests lies the shadow of the violent conflict between the Taira and the Minamoto.

Q: Why do the Japanese like to eat at food stalls?

A: Outdoor carts and stands that sell *ramen* are popular even with young women. High school and college girls, who normally avoid restaurants that cater to middle-aged men, are willing to rub shoulders with older men at food stands.

According to one account, the source of the widespread popularity of food carts dates back to the samurai era. During the Warring States period, fighting men were told to

そのため、食べたり排泄するのは、短時間で
すますのが基本。武士にとっては、早飯が当た
り前だったのである。
　この習慣が一般にも広まって、江戸時代には、
早く食事をすませる屋台や天秤棒をかついだ売
り子が街にあふれていた。

　夜泣きそば屋や焼きいも売りもそうだし、寿
司屋も昔は屋台のものだった。
　とくに、武士と同じ威勢のよさと、気風が売
りの江戸っ子には、早飯のできる屋台がピッタ
リ。それが現在にも受け継がれているのは、要
するに日本人はいまも昔も早飯の国民だという
ことだ。
　また、気取りやぜいたくとは無縁の世界なの
も、人気の理由だろう。
　屋台に、ひんぱんに足を運ぶ人は、たいてい
落ち着いて食事するフランス料理や京懐石が嫌
いなタイプではなかろうか？

"eat fast, shit fast, and prepare fast." Soldiers must be ready to fight at any time.

Thus the fundamental principle was to eat and perform other bodily functions in a short time. Eating quickly was part of the samurai's job.

The custom of eating quickly became widespread. In the Edo period, fast-food carts and children selling food from baskets suspended from shoulder poles were common sights in cities and towns.

Yonaki soba and baked sweet-potato sellers follow in the same tradition. Even sushi was a stall food many years ago.

For natives of Tokyo, the dashing spirit and disposition of the samurai were valued, so food carts that allowed quick eating were perfect. The continued popularity of the carts shows that Japan has always been a nation of rapid eaters.

The popularity of the carts is also helped by the complete lack of pretension and luxury.

People who often eat at food carts are unlikely to appreciate the slow relaxed style of French or Kyoto *kaiseki* cuisine.

Q: 日本には、なぜ「三」のつくことわざが多いのか？

A: ──────「石の上にも三年」「仏の顔も三度」「三人寄れば文殊の知恵」「早起きは三文の徳」「二度あることは三度ある」「三つ子の魂百まで」などなど、日本には「三」のつくことわざが多い。

これは、「三」という数字には二面性があるためだ。「三」は、あるときは「少ない」「短い」という意味になり、あるときは「多い」「長い」という意味になる。

たとえば、「三日坊主」「二束三文」というのは、「短い」「少ない」という意味のほうの「三」。一方、「石の上にも三年」「馬鹿の三杯汁（馬鹿の大食い）」の「三」は、「長い」「多い」の意味合いをもつ。

CHAPTER 7

Trivia on
Japanese Language

Q: Why are there so many Japanese proverbs that use the number three?

A: The number three appears in many Japanese proverbs: "three years on a stone" (meaning if you sit three years on a cold stone, it will eventually get warm, thus showing the value of persistence); "three times in Buddha's face" (even Buddha will get angry if you slap his face three times); "if three people are together, they have the wisdom of Bodhisattva Manjusri"; "waking early is worth three *mon* (an old unit of currency)"; "if something happens twice, it will happen three times"; "the spirit of the three-year-old is the same at one hundred"; and many more.

The popularity of three comes from the number's dual nature. Sometimes three means "a few" or "short," and sometimes it means "many" or "long."

For example, in the expressions "a three-day priest," meaning someone who attempts something and soon quits, or "two bundles for three *mon*," meaning a large quantity sold for a low price, three means "a few, short." However, in "three years on a stone" or "the fool's three

また、日本では昔から「三」が神聖な数、縁起のいい数とされ、神話のなかにも「三世界（高天原、黄泉の国、現の国）」「三種の神器」といった言葉が出てくるし、「七五三」「三三九度」などの儀式にも「三」の数字が用いられる。

さらに、「三」は「満つ、充つ」に通じるめでたい数字でもあり、ことわざではないが、「三拍子そろう」「御三家」「三大〇〇」といった具合につかわれることも多い。

というわけで、日本人は昔からことわざにかぎらず、「三」という数字を好んでつかっているのだ。

Q: 日本には、なぜ「鈴木」という名字が多いのか？

A: ———— 日本人の姓に関する調査では、たいていが鈴木、佐藤が1位、2位を占めることになる。

「鈴木」という名前は、日本人が農耕民族であったことの証明ともいえる名前だ。中世にできた名前で、もともとの読みはススキ。その昔、刈り取った稲を田に積み上げ、その上に1本の棒を立てて神を呼ぶ神事が行われていた。

そのときの棒をススキといい、鈴木の文字には聖木の意味があったのだ。最初は、米の増産

bowls" (indicating gluttony), three means "many, long."

Since ancient times, the number three has also been a sacred number, an indicator of good fortune. Japanese myths tell of the "three worlds" (heaven, the land of the dead, and the world we live in) and the "three sacred objects" of the imperial throne. Three also appears in the ceremonies given for seven-, five-, and three-year-old children and the wedding tradition of drinking three times from each of three cups.

One word for three in Japanese, *mitsu*, is homophonous with words meaning "full" or "replete," so the number is also regarded as auspicious. Nonproverbial idioms using three (also pronounced *san*) include *sanbyōshi sorou* (all three requirements met), *go-sanke* (three prominent people in a particular field), and *sandai naninani* (the three big something-or-other).

Thus since ancient times the Japanese have, in proverbs and otherwise, liked the number three.

Q: Why is the surname Suzuki so common in Japan?

A: Surveys of Japanese surnames usually show Suzuki to be the most common, followed in second place by Satō.

The surname Suzuki shows that the Japanese used to be an agricultural people. The name originated in the Middle Ages, when it was pronounced Susuki. In those days, when harvested rice stalks were stacked in a field, a stick was placed on top of each stack in a ceremony for calling to the gods. That stick was called a *susuki*, and the surname Suzuki came from that sacred stick. The first person to adopt

にかかわる熊野の神官が鈴木の姓を名のり、熊野信仰の影響で、鈴木姓が庶民のあいだに広がっていった。

まさに豊作を願う日本人の、農耕民族たることを表した名字が鈴木なのである。

一方の佐藤は、藤原氏系の姓。由来には2つあり、左衛門尉公清を祖として佐藤、または左藤とする説、藤原秀郷（ひでさと）が下野国佐野庄を本拠地として勢力をはったので佐藤とする説がそれだ。

Q: 日本人の名前には、なぜ珍名が多いのか？

A: ———— 日本には12万種もの名字があるという。それに比べ、同じ漢字圏で人口11億を有する中国がたったの5,000種、韓国が249種。

多くの民族が混在するヨーロッパでさえ、全体で6万種というから、日本の名字がいかに多いか、おわかりだろう。

日本で、農民や町民が名字をもつことを許されたのは、明治3年（1870年）のことだった。しかし、当時の庶民の生活には名字をもつ必要性がなく、八百屋の八っつぁん、魚屋の熊さんなどの呼び名がありさえすれば、それで十分だった。

したがって、名字の届け出をしたのは僧侶ぐらいのもので、あとの庶民は、「名字をつける

Suzuki as a surname was a Shinto priest in Kumano whose job was to boost rice harvests. As the Kumano faith spread, the name became popular among the common folk.

The Suzuki surname is thus proof of the Japanese people's origin as farmers who prayed for good harvests.

The number-two name, Satō, comes from the powerful Fujiwara family. The *kanji* for *fuji* in Fujiwara is also pronounced *tō*, the last syllable of Satō. The syllable *sa* is said to come either from an ancestor who had the bureaucratic title *saemon no jō* or from the place name Sano in the old province of Shimotsuke, where Fujiwara no Hidesato had his base of operations.

Q: Why are there so many unusual Japanese surnames?

A: There are said to be some 120,000 Japanese surnames. This is surprising compared to the 5,000 surnames among the 1.1 billion Chinese and the 249 surnames in Korea, the other two countries that have family names written in Chinese characters.

Even among the many nationalities of Europe there are only a total of 60,000 family names. This shows how vast the number of Japanese surnames is.

Japanese farmers and townsfolk were allowed to use surnames beginning in 1870. But even then, most common people had no need for a second name. It was good enough to have a nickname, such as "Yattsan of the *yaoya* (grocer's)" or "Kuma-san of the fish shop."

About the only people who signed up for surnames were Buddhist priests. Other commoners viewed the idea

なんてどこの世界の話だ?」という感じだった。

　だが、一日も早く近代国家の体裁を整えたい政府は、庶民の無関心にいら立ち、「平民名字必称義務令」を布告。これにあわてた庶民は、僧侶や庄屋に頼んで名字をつけてもらったが、かぎられた時間で多くの名前をつけるのはむずかしく、書物から拝借したり、野菜や魚や鳥などから名前をとったりした。そのせいで珍名が続々と生まれることになった。

　浜地<ruby>浜地<rt>はまち</rt></ruby>さん、太古<ruby>太古<rt>たこ</rt></ruby>さん……あなたの周囲にも、1人くらいは変わった名字の友人知人がいませんか。

Q: 日本語は、外国人にとってなぜヒアリングしにくいのか?

A: ─────外国人に日本語の印象を聞くと、「さ」「よ」「ね」の3音が非常に多くつかわれているような感じがするという。日本語では、語尾がこれらの音で終わることが多いためと、分析される。

　さて、外国人には、「日本語のヒアリングはむずかしい」という人が多い。その最大の理由は、日本語に強弱のアクセントがほとんどないことがあげられる。強弱のアクセントがないぶん、めりはりのない言葉に聞こえ、単語と単語の区別がつきにくくなり、意味がとれなくなるのだ。

　逆に、日本語以外の言葉、とくに欧米系の言語は、強弱のアクセントが中心になっている。アクセントのある音を特別に強く発音し、その反面、アクセントのない音は小さく発音し、ときには発音しない。

of having a surname almost as a joke.

The Japanese government, though, was eager to turn Japan into a modern nation. Annoyed at the lack of interest in surnames, it issued an order requiring everyone to adopt a family name. People then rushed to their priests or village elders to get a name assigned. However, it was difficult to come up with so many names in a limited time, so they just grabbed words out of books or used the names of vegetables, fish, or birds. That's why so many unusual names were created.

You may have a Japanese friend or acquaintance with a strange name, a Hamachi-san ("Ms. Yellowtail Tuna"), perhaps, or a Tako-san ("Mr. Octopus").

Q: Why is spoken Japanese so hard for foreigners to understand?

A: When foreigners are asked their impression of the Japanese language, they say that the syllables *so*, *yo*, and *ne* are used extremely often. This can be explained by the fact that sentences in spoken Japanese often end with these sounds.

Many foreigners say that Japanese is difficult to understand when it is spoken. The main reason is that Japanese has almost no distinction between strongly stressed and weakly stressed syllables. This lack of stress makes the language sound monotonous. One word is difficult to tell from another, so it is hard to catch the meaning.

Most other languages, especially those of Europe, have distinct syllabic stresses. Accented syllables are pronounced very strongly, while unaccented syllables are said weakly or not at all.

たとえば、「ホットドッグ（Hot dog）」を、日本人はすべての音を同じ強さで発音する。一方、英語では前のOに強いアクセントを置き、「ハッダッ」というような感じで発音する。子音のtとgをほとんど発音しないわけだ。

いいかえれば、外国人が日本語をヒアリングしにくい理由は、日本人が外国語をヒアリングできない理由と同じだといえる。日本人が欧米系言語の発音をマスターするには、強弱アクセントが最大の壁になる。

Q: 日本語には、なぜ「私」「俺」などの人称代名詞が多いのか？

A: ──────── 英語を初めて学んだとき、「I」を「私」、「YOU」を「あなた」と訳すことに抵抗はなかっただろうか？

「私」はともかく、「あなた」という言葉を中学生がつかうことはめったにない。「おまえ」とか「あんた」がふつうで、「きみ」をつかうのは優等生タイプ、「てめえ」はやや不良っぽい中学生がつかい、アニメの好きなマニアタイプは「おたく」というだろう。

一人称のほうにしたって、男の子の場合、ふつうは「僕」か「俺」である。「わし」「自分」「あたし」「あたい」と呼ぶこともあるだろう。

ことほどさように、日本語の人称代名詞は、外国語に比べるとひじょうに数が多い。そのいちばん大きな理由は、敬語との関係だ。

日本人は昔から、自分と相手の身分関係、人

Take, for example, the word "hot dog." When Japanese people say it, they pronounce each sound with the same stress. In English, though, the first *o* receives a stronger accent than the second. To Japanese ears, that pronunciation sounds like *hod*, with the consonants *t* and *g* barely audible.

In other words, the reason foreigners have a hard time understanding spoken Japanese is the same reason Japanese can't understand other languages. The biggest barrier to mastery of European languages by the Japanese is syllabic stress.

Q: Why does Japanese have so many personal pronouns?

A: When the Japanese first study English in junior high school, they often hesitate to translate "I" as the first-person pronoun *watashi* and "you" as the second-person pronoun *anata*. Though children of that age might use the word *watashi*, they seldom call others *anata*. Instead, they're more likely to use the less formal *omae* or *anta*. Goody-goody students call each other *kimi*, while the tougher kids use the coarser *temē*. Nerdy types who like cartoons say *otaku*.

When referring to themselves, boys usually say *boku* or *ore*. Other variants for "I" include *washi*, *jibun*, *atashi*, and *atai*.

Thus Japanese has a much larger number of personal pronouns than other languages. The main reason for this glut is the use of honorific language.

Since ancient times, the people have used different per-

間関係を示すために、一人称をつかい分けてきたのだ。

　昔の人は、自分と相手の関係によって、「ここもと」「てまえ」「拙者」「小生」「貴殿」「そちら」「おまえ様」「尊下」などをつかい分け、現在の私たちも、「私」「俺」「僕」「きみ」「あなた」「おまえ」などをつかい分ける。

　また現代では、言葉の流行りすたりのスピードが増しているために、人称代名詞の数が増えているともいえる。「おたく」は、その最たる例だ。

Q: なぜ日本の国名は「日本」というのか？

A: ────── 中国や朝鮮の古い記録では、日本は「倭」と記されている。その「倭」を「和」と変え、上に「大」をつけて「大和」と自称するようになった。

　その大和が「日本」になったのは、7世紀の初頭、中国や朝鮮との位置関係から、「日出ずる処」（『隋書倭国伝』）と、自ら名のったことに由来する。

　やがて、ヒノモト（日の本）が、万葉集などで大和国の枕詞として用いられるようになり、8世紀に入ってすぐに施行された大宝律令で、天皇を対外的に「天神御宇日本天皇」と呼ぶことを規定した。これが、「日本」という

sonal pronouns depending on their social and personal relationship to the people they are speaking to.

Long ago, people would choose between *kokomoto*, *temē*, *sessha*, *shōsei*, and others terms to refer to themselves, and *kiden*, *sochira*, *omae*, and *sonka* to refer to others. The choice depended on the relationship between the speaker and the listener. Today, the Japanese discriminate similarly between *watashi*, *ore*, *boku*, and other terms for "I," and *kimi*, *anata*, *omae*, etc., for "you."

Vogue words are adopted and abandoned with increasing speed in Japan, and the number of personal pronouns is also increasing. The best recent example is *otaku*, a relatively new word for "you."

Q: Why is Japan called both *Nihon* or *Nippon* in Japanese?

A: In old histories from China and Korea, Japan is referred to by the character 倭, which is read *wa* in Japanese. Later 倭 was replaced by the homophonous 和, and the character 大 ("big") was prefixed to it to give 大和, which is pronounced *yamato*.

The people of Yamato adopted the characters 日本, literally "sun origin," for the name of their country because Yamato was referred to as the "land of the rising sun" in the seventh-century Chinese travel report *Zuisho Wakoku-den*. That name was chosen because Japan was in the direction of the sunrise as viewed from China and Korea. In the *Man'yōshū* and other early poetry collections, the phrase *Hi no moto*, which also means "origin of the sun," was used as a conventional term for Yamato, and the Taihō Code

名前のはじまりである。

　奈良時代には、この「日本」を依然として「やまと」、あるいは「ひのもと」と読んでいたが、やがて漢字の知識が広がるにつれて、「にほむ」と発音されるようになったようだ。「にほん」「にっぽん」という発音が生まれたのは、さらに時代が下って室町時代に入ってからのことである。

　それからずって後の昭和9年（1934年）、文部省の臨時国語調査会で、「日本」の読みを「にっぽん」に統一することが決まり、戦時中にかけては、この読み方が強制された。音感からいくと、「にほん」と読むほうが、より日本語らしいのだが、軍事国へと突きすすんでいた当時、「にっぽん」のほうが力強くていい、ということだったらしい。

　ちなみに、大昔の日本は「大八島」「豊葦原瑞穂国」「葦原中国」などとも呼ばれた。緑の稲穂が垂れる、豊かな田園の日本の原風景が思い浮かべられるような、何とも風情のある名前ではないか。

Q: 日本はなぜ英語でジャパンと呼ばれるようになったのか？

A: ──────── 日本を英語でジャパン（Japan）というのは、中国語の「ジッポン」からきている。現在の中国語の標準語といわれる北京語では、日本は

adopted in the early eighth century required that the Japanese emperor be called by a title that included the characters 日本. Thus 日本 became the name of Japan.

In the Nara period, the characters were still read as *Yamato* or *Hi no moto*. As more people became literate, the pronunciation *Nihomu* was adopted as well. It wasn't until the Muromachi period that the name came to be pronounced either *Nihon* or *Nippon* as it is today.

Much later, in 1934, a special language commission of the Ministry of Education decided that only one reading, *Nippon*, should be used, and that reading was required until the end of World War II. While the pronunciation *Nihon* seems more typically Japanese, *Nippon* sounded tougher and stronger for a country that was then becoming increasingly militaristic.

In ancient times, Japan was also called *Ōyashima*, "The Great Eight Islands," *Toyoashihara no Mizuho no Kuni*, "Country of the Rich Fields of Reeds and Rice," and *Ashihara no Nakatsu Kuni*, "Middle Country of the Reed Fields." These expressive names evoked picturesque Japanese landscape of verdant rice plants and lush fields.

Q: Why is the country called "Japan" in English?

A: The English word "Japan" comes from the old Chinese name for the country, *Jihpun*. In Mandarin, the standard Beijing dialect of Chinese, the characters for Japan are pronounced

「リーベン」と発音されるが、中国南部では、いまでも「ジッパン」「ジーベン」「ジッポン」などと発音するところがある。

では、中国語の「ジッポン」がどうして英語の「ジャパン」につながったかというと、日本を黄金の国と紹介したマルコ・ポーロの『東方見聞録』のおかげである。マルコ・ポーロは「ジッポン」の発音を「ジパング」と聴き覚え記録した。それが世界中に広まったというわけだ。

したがって、日本を表すドイツ語の「ヤーパン」、スペイン語の「ハポン」なども、いずれも出所は『東方見聞録』。最初の発音が違うのは、Ｊの発音の違いからである。

Q: なぜ、「日本語が日本人をつくりだす」といわれるか？

A: ──── まず、大脳生理学の初歩から。

「人間の脳には右脳と左脳の2つがあり、右脳が直観とパターン認識、左脳が言語と理論的思考をつかさどっている」──ここまでは、ご存じの方も多いと思う。

さて、問題はここから。日本人は、この右脳と左脳を特殊なつかい方をしていることがわかってきたのだ。日本人はほかの人種に比べて、左脳を酷使しているのだという。

たとえば、虫の鳴き声、楽器音などを、日本人は左脳で処理している。一方、西欧人は、言語以外の音は、右脳で対応する。

Riben. In southern China, though, pronunciations like *Jipan*, *Jiben*, or *Jipon* are still used.

The Chinese *Jihpun* became the English "Japan" thanks to *The Travels of Marco Polo*, which described Japan as a country of gold. In that book, Marco called Japan *Zipangu*, which is how the word sounded to him. That name was then adapted by other languages. The German *Japan*, pronounced *"yapan,"* and the Spanish *Japón*, pronounced *"hapon,"* originate as well in Marco Polo's *Travels*. The difference in pronunciation is due to the different ways the letter *j* is pronounced.

Q: Why do people say that it is the Japanese language that makes Japanese people?

A: First, let's start with a brief introduction to cerebral physiology.

The human brain is divided into two lobes, the left and right. The right brain is used for direct perception and pattern recognition, while the left brain is in charge of language and logical thinking. Many readers probably know this much already.

It's also known that Japanese people use their right and left brains in a unique way. The Japanese use their left brains much more intensely than people of other ethnic groups.

For example, the Japanese process insect chirps and the sounds of musical instruments with their left brains. Westerners use their right brains for such nonlinguistic sounds.

なぜ、こんなことが起こるかというと、理由の1つとして、「日本語では、音をすべて擬音化し、言葉としてとらえてしまうからではないか」というのが有力な仮説になってきている。たとえば、鈴虫の鳴き声を、日本人は環境音としてでなく、「リンリン」という言葉としてとらえているというわけだ。

　この仮説の有力な傍証として、日本語のできない日系人のケースがあげられる。そういう日系人の脳は、西欧人パターンを示すのだ。つまり、虫の鳴き声などは右脳でとらえるわけだ。ここから、日本人の脳そのものが特殊なのではなく、日本語をつかううちに日本人の脳は特殊になっていくという結論が導きだされるわけだ。

　いずれにせよ、日本人が左脳をつかいすぎているのは、確かなことだ。いわば、左脳は満杯状態になっているわけで、これが日本人の外国語下手の理由の1つになっているとも考えられている。

Q: なぜ、江戸のあの橋を「日本橋」というようになったか？

A: ─────── ♪お江戸日本橋七つ立ち〜、と幕末から明治にかけて流行した歌にも歌われた日本橋は、現在も東京の地名として残っている。

　この日本橋、徳川家康が征夷大将軍に任ぜられた慶長8年（1603年）に架設されたもので、長さ68メートル、幅7メートルもあるものだった。その時代としては、江戸のシンボルともい

One likely hypothesis for this is that, in Japanese, all sounds are interpreted as words through a kind of onomatopoeia. For example, the crying of a cicada is heard by the Japanese not as just another background noise but as the word *rinrin*.

Strong corroboration for this hypothesis comes from people of Japanese ancestry who cannot speak Japanese. Their brains exhibit the same patterns as those of Westerners: they process insect chirps and similar sounds through their right brains. This leads to the conclusion that the brains of Japanese people are not special, only the brains of those who speak Japanese.

In any case, it's clear that Japanese people use their left brains too much. And that's one reason why Japanese are poor at foreign languages: their left brains are already packed to capacity.

Q: Why is the bridge in central Edo (Tokyo) called Nihonbashi?

A: "Leaving Nihonbashi in Edo at four in the morning...." Those were the lyrics of a song popular in the late Edo and early Meiji periods. The name Nihonbashi—literally, "Japan Bridge"—is still used in Tokyo today.

The original bridge was built on the order of Shogun Tokugawa Ieyasu in 1603. Sixty-eight meters long and seven meters wide, the bridge was a magnificent symbol of Edo at that time.

えるくらい立派な橋だったのだ。

　一方、現在の日本橋は長さ49メートルで幅27メートル、明治44年（1911年）に架設されている。また、あまり知られていないが、橋にかかる「日本橋」の文字は、徳川慶喜の筆によるものだ。

　ところで、日本橋の名前の由来だが、日本を代表する橋だから日本橋かと思うと、そうではないようだ。『慶長見聞集』では、「この橋が日本橋と呼ばれるようになったのはまったく不思議なこと」とある。つまり由来がわからないというわけだが、一説によると、2本の木を渡した橋だから二本橋で、それが日本橋になったといわれる。

　ともかく、橋の名前をつけたのは、お上でも特定の人物でもなく、誰かがそれを日本橋と呼び、それがいつの間にか橋の名前として定着したものであるようだ。

Q: 日本のあの名曲が、なぜ、アメリカでは『スキヤキ』になったのか？

A: ──── 機会があればアメリカに進出しようと考えている日本人歌手は少なくない。日本での知名度がいくらあっても、アメリカではまったく無名の歌手として一からスタートしなくてはならない。やる気とチャレンジ精神はむろんのこと、相当な実力がないとなかなか通用しない世界だ。

　そこへいくと、全米ナンバーワンのヒット曲歌手となった坂本九は、正真正銘、実力で1位を勝ちとったのだから、見事なものだ。なにし

The present bridge, 49 meters long and 27 meters wide, was built in 1911. Few people know that the inscription showing the bridge's name was modeled after the calligraphy of Tokugawa Yoshinobu, the last shogun.

The name Nihonbashi suggests that the bridge was named to symbolize Japan, but that doesn't seem to be true. An account from the early Edo period states: "It's surprising that this bridge came to be called Nihonbashi." The source of the name is unknown. According to one explanation, the name comes from the fact that two trees were used to make the span—"two trees" being *nihon no ki* in Japanese.

In any case, the bridge was not named by any powerful or specific person. Rather, someone just started calling it Nihonbashi and the name eventually stuck.

Q: Why was the Japanese hit song called "Sukiyaki" in the United States?

A: Many Japanese pop singers would like to work in the United States if they had a chance. No matter how famous performers are in Japan, they have to start from scratch as unknowns in America. And to succeed in the American entertainment business, they need not only enthusiasm and ambition but a high degree of talent as well.

Thus the number-one hit of the singer Sakamato Kyū is all the more impressive because it shows his real ability. Two years after his *Ue o Muite Arukō* ("Let's Walk While

ろ日本国内でヒットした2年後、『上を向いて歩こう』のタイトルを『スキヤキ』に変えただけで、日本語のオリジナル盤のまま発売された曲が、レスリー・ゴーアの『涙のバースデイ・パーティー』を抑えて全米ナンバーワンにランクされたのだ。

この時期、ビーチ・ボーイズの『サーフィンUSA』やPPMの『パフ』などがヒットチャートをにぎわせていたのだから、『スキヤキ』の1位はまさに偉業といえるだろう。

ところで、『スキヤキ』というタイトルだが、イギリスのジャズメン、ケニー・ボールがインスト曲としてレコーディングした際につけたもので、長い原題ではイギリスのDJたちが発音できないので、彼らが知っている数少ない日本語のなかから、このタイトルが選ばれた。

このケニー・ボール盤も、全米チャートで10位にランク。当時、スキヤキという言葉は、ますます知名度をあげ、外国人の知るもっともポピュラーな日本語になった。

Looking Up") was a hit in Japan, it reached the top of the charts in the U.S. in its original Japanese version; only the title was changed to "Sukiyaki." It beat out Lesley Gore's "It's My Party" and grabbed the number-one spot on the U.S. charts.

Considering that competing hits at that time included the Beach Boys' "Surfin' USA" and Peter, Paul and Mary's "Puff the Magic Dragon," the success of "Sukiyaki" was truly a significant achievement.

The title "Sukiyaki" was given to the song when an instrumental version was recorded by English jazz musician Kenny Ball. English disk jockeys were unable to pronounce the long Japanese name, so one of the few Japanese words that DJs would know was chosen instead.

Kenny Ball's version made it to number ten on the U.S. charts. The word "sukiyaki" became so well known as a result that it was the most familiar Japanese word to foreigners at that time.

第8章 日本の「弱点」の雑学

Q: 日本人は、なぜキスが下手なのか？

A: ────── 日本人がやってもサマにならないものに、キスがある。駅の改札口近くなどで、キスをするカップルを見かけることがあるが、これがカッコ悪い。欧米人のキスは、さわやかな雰囲気だが、日本人のキスは、何となくヒワイな感じがある。

日本人がキス下手なのは、その歴史が浅いからだろうが、昔の日本人があまりキスをしなかったのは、「口はけがれているもの」と考えていたからだという。たとえば、日本人は、大皿の料理には取り箸をつける。家族といえども、口につけるものが交わらないようにしてきたわけだ。

文献に、キスが表れるのは、室町時代以降。それまでは、愛情表現のキスをしていたかどうかは疑問とされている。もっとも、平安時代の衣冠束帯と十二単衣を着ると、2人のあいだでは50センチも離れ、唇は届かなかったのではないかという意見もあるが、昔から、日本人はキスに少し抵抗があったようだ。

CHAPTER 8

Trivia on
Japan's Downsides

Q: Why are the Japanese so bad at kissing?

A: Something that the Japanese can't do well even if they try is kissing. Sometimes you see couples in Japan kissing at places like train station entrances, but they look gross. When Westerners kiss, it looks wholesome. When Japanese kiss, it looks obscene.

One reason Japanese are so bad at this is that the practice is still relatively new. Japanese people seldom kissed in former times because the mouth was thought to be impure. Even today, when a shared dish is placed on the table, a separate pair of serving chopsticks is provided. Even in a family, people don't like to share food that has been in contact with somebody else's mouth.

The first appearances of kissing in written records date from the Muromachi period or later. Until then, it is doubtful whether people ever kissed as a sign of affection. When nobles of the Heian period wore outer kimono over their bulky formal clothes, people would have to stand as much as 50 centimeters apart! According to some accounts, their lips could not even touch. In any case, the Japanese

欧米人のように、さわやかなキスができるま
でには、まだまだ時間が必要かもしれない。

　ちなみに、欧米のキスにはいろいろな種類が
あって、親愛のキスは両手を広げて軽く抱き合
い、相手の頬にチュッとする。また、称賛のキ
スは相手の額、料理をほめるときは頬、尊敬の
キスは手の甲にする。

Q: なぜ、日本人には肩こりが多いのか?

A: ――――肩こりは、緊張やストレス、目の疲れから起こ
る。いつもリラックスを心がける欧米人に比べ、
「がんばろう」と緊張しやすい日本人は、それ
だけ肩がこりやすいといわれている。

　また、欧米人に比べ、日本人は姿勢が悪いし、
手や腕をつかうとき、肩の筋肉を動かすのが下
手だ。そのため、肩の筋肉がかたまりやすく、
肩こりになりやすいとも考えられる。

　もっとも、最近、アメリカに「ニンテンド
ウ・ネック」という造語ができた。意味は「肩
こり」だが、「ネック(首)」と呼ぶのは、英語
で、首のつけ根あたりは「首」だから。コンピ
ュータゲームをして、肩がこったときにつかう
言葉である。つまり、最近まで、アメリカに
「肩こり」という言葉はなかったのだが、これ
まで、アメリカ人が肩こりを感じなかったのは、
「肩こり」に当たる言葉がなかったからではな
いかともいわれている。

seem to have some resistance to kissing ever since ancient times.

It will be a long time before the Japanese can kiss as easily and as wholesomely as Westerners.

In the West, there are many types of kissing. To show affection, people spread their arms, embrace lightly, and peck each other's cheek. To show approval, they kiss the forehead. To praise food, they kiss the cheek. And to show respect, they kiss the back of the hand.

Q: Why do many Japanese suffer from stiff shoulders?

A: Stiff Shoulders—or *katakori*—is caused by tension, stress, and tired eyes. While Westerners try to stay relaxed, the fighting spirit of the Japanese tends to make them tense up, resulting in stiff shoulders.

The Japanese also do not have good posture compared to Westerners. When using the hands or arms, Japanese don't know how to move their shoulder muscles. The muscles easily tighten, resulting in stiffness.

Recently a new term has appeared in America, "Nintendo neck." It refers to the cramped neck and shoulders suffered by people playing computer games. Previously, there was no word in English that corresponded to *katakori* in Japanese. Perhaps that's why Americans never complained of the problem.

じっさい、筋肉のこり具合をみる検査で、「肩はこらない」といっていたアメリカ女性が、肩こりを訴えた日本女性よりこっていたという報告もある。昔から、「肩こり」という言葉のある日本人は、意識するため、よけいに肩こりを感じていたといえるかもしれない。

Q: 日本の天気予報は、なぜ当てにくいのか？

A: ──── 天気予報がはずれると、気象庁に抗議の電話をかける人が多いという。「予報」なんだから、はずれても仕方がない、とはいかない。何にでも完全を求める日本人には、ひと言文句をいわないと気がすまないという人が多いということか。

しかし、現実に日本の天気を予測するのは世界一むずかしいという。たとえば、大陸型のヨーロッパでは、気圧配置は安定的で、天気もあまり変わらない。晴れなら、晴れが1週間ぐらい続くのがふつうである。

それに比べ、島国の日本は、ユーラシア大陸と、太平洋からの寒気団や湿った空気の影響をまともに受ける。そのため、とくに春や晩秋はめまぐるしく天気が変わることも珍しくない。だから、天気予報も、きわめてむずかしくなってしまうわけだ。気象庁でも、「晴れ」の予報で雨が降るとまずいが、「晴れ」の予報で曇りなら、「まずまずの予報」と、採点はかなり甘くなっているという。

ところが、国民はそうではない。日替わり天気となるから、そのぶん毎日、天気予報を気に

According to one study of muscle stiffness, American women who said that they didn't suffer from stiff shoulders actually had stiffer muscles than did Japanese women who complained of *katakori*. Perhaps the Japanese, who have had a word for the problem for generations, are more aware of it and so suffer from it more than others.

Q: Why are Japanese weather forecasts so frequently wrong?

A: When a weather forecast is wrong, many people call the Meteorological Agency to complain. They don't accept the fact that incorrect forecasts are inevitable. Perfectionists in everything, the Japanese feel compelled to criticize.

In fact, though, the weather in Japan is said to be the hardest in the world to predict. On a continent like Europe, for example, the air pressure zones are stable and the weather doesn't change much. If it's clear, it's likely to stay clear for a week.

In contrast, the islands of Japan are strongly affected by both cold air masses from Eurasia and humid air from the Pacific Ocean. That's why sudden weather changes are so common in spring and late autumn, thus making it very difficult to predict the weather accurately. The Meteorological Agency isn't happy if it predicts fair weather and it rains, but if the weather is cloudy they will be content that the forecast was at least moderately correct. The agency does not hold itself to very high standards.

The people of Japan, though, are not so easy-going. Since the weather is different every day, they pay attention

して、当たりはずれにますます敏感になる。

　たしかに、毎日の天気予報が「晴れ。ところにより雷雨」というタイのような国では、台風が発生したとき以外、天気予報を気にする人はいない。晴れていてもスコールがあるのがふつうだから、天気の心配という悩みもないのである。

Q: 日本の地下鉄は、なぜ乗り換えが不便なのか？

A: ──────東京で地下鉄を乗り換えるため、表示に従って歩くと、やたら歩かされることがある。東京に住む人間でもそうだから、地方からきて路線図を見ながら移動する人は、つい「ふう」とため息をつくことが多いと思う。

　地下鉄の乗り換えが不便なのは、もともと将来のことをなにも考えずに、いきあたりばったりで工事をすすめてきたからである。
　ヨーロッパの地下鉄は、最初から路線の接続を念頭に入れて設計されている。将来、こういう路線が必要になれば、この駅を乗り換え駅にする……といったことをあらかじめ考えてつくってある。また、急に新路線を通すことになっても、既存の駅を含めて再検討。乗り換えがうまくいくように、設計されるのである。
　それに比べ、日本の地下鉄、とくに東京の地下鉄は、あとのことを考えてこなかった。そのため、新しい路線をつくると、中途半端な場所に駅ができることになる。その結果、地下街を

to forecasts each day and are very sensitive to whether or not the predictions are accurate.

In a country like Thailand, where every day the forecast is "sunny with scattered thunderstorms," few people pay attention to weather reports except when a typhoon is coming. It's normal to have squalls even when the sky is clear, so nobody worries about the weather.

Q: Why do Japanese subways have such inconvenient transfers?

A: When you change trains on the Tokyo subways, you'll often find yourself forced to follow the signs a long way as you walk from one train line to the next. Tokyo residents are not exempt from these treks, so people visiting from the provinces are even more likely to feel exhausted as they switch trains with their eyes glued to their route maps.

Transfers on Tokyo subways are so inconvenient because the train lines were built without any foresight or planning.

In Europe, subways are designed from the beginning with connections in mind. The designers think, "If we need a line here in the future, this can be the transfer station." And if a new line is built without such prior planning, they re-evaluate the whole system, including existing stations. The lines are designed for easy transfers.

In Japan, though, and especially in Tokyo, no thought is given to the future. That's why stations on new lines are in such awkward locations. Passengers are forced to walk through long underground passages and go up and down

長く歩かされたり、長い階段を上り下りさせられたりしてしまうのである。

さらにいえば、東京の地下は、水道管や下水道、ガス管が縦横無尽に走っていて、手がつけられなくなっている。これも、計画なしに埋め、つぎつぎと継ぎ足していったからだが、そのため新しい地下鉄は、より深いところを通すしかなく、駅と駅が上下にも離れてしまうのである。

最初がいきあたりばったりだから、いまごろ苦労する。地下鉄の乗り換えの悪さは、何事も「最初が肝心」という素朴な教訓を改めて教えてくれる。

Q: 日本の公衆便所は、なぜ欧米人に評判が悪いのか？

A: ──────欧米からの旅行者が、閉口するものの1つに、日本の公衆便所がある。なにが不満なのかと聞くと、男子トイレで、外から小便している姿が見えることががまんならないという。

そういわれれば、日本の公衆便所には、外から、男性が便器にむかって並んでいるのが見えるところが多い。この便所のつくり方に、欧米人は「無神経」と閉口してしまうのである。

こういうと、欧米の男子トイレの「大」のほうは、扉の下から入っている人の脚が見える。あれこそ、無神経なつくりと反論したい人もいるかもしれない。

しかし欧米の人には、便所のなかで見える姿は許せるというのである。彼らは、「大」でも「小」でも、便所に入れば、排泄するという同

lengthy stairways.

The situation is made even worse by the vast tangle of water mains, sewers, and gas pipes that crisscross subterranean Tokyo. These utility lines were installed and connected without any planning, and new subway lines have to be dug deep enough to go under them. That's why subways stations are often at such different levels.

The lack of planning in the beginning means that we all suffer now. The bad arrangement of subway transfers in Japan only reconfirms the importance of getting started on the right foot.

Q: Why do Westerners dislike public restrooms in Japan?

A: One thing that visitors from Europe or America can't stand in Japan are public restrooms. If you ask them why, they'll tell you it's because people standing outside men's restrooms can see the men inside.

It's true that men lined up in front of urinals are often visible from outside. That way of designing restrooms is what drives Westerners up the wall.

In the West, though, the stalls in men's restrooms allow the user's legs to be seen from outside. You'd think people would object to that even more.

But Westerners don't mind being seen by others inside the restroom. They figure that everybody in a restroom is there for the same purpose, whether at the urinal or in the

じ目的をもった、いわば仲間。その姿が、お互いに少しぐらい見えても気にならない。

　ところが、便所の外にいる人は、排泄する意志がない。そんな無関係な人に、便所のなかの姿を見られることを極端に嫌うのである。

　こういうのをカルチャーギャップというのだろうが、欧米人のこの感覚、ちょっと理解できない人が多いかもしれない。

Q: なぜ、日本には「登山」というスポーツがなかったのか？

A: ──────── エベレストを目指す日本の登山家は多い。しかし、日本は山の多い国のわりに、登山というスポーツが登場したのは、ようやく1900年代に入ってからのことである。

　ヨーロッパで登山が流行するのは1700年代だから、ずいぶん遅れている。もちろん、鎖国時代だったこともあるが、それ以上に日本人が登山をしようと思わなかったのは、当時の人たちがもっていた山に対するイメージに原因がある。

　日本では、山は信仰と結びついて「霊場」と呼ばれ、山伏、修験者が修行をする聖なる場所と考えられていたのだ。そのため、一般の人々にとって、山は畏敬の場所。畏れ多くて登ろうなどとは考えなかったのだ。明治維新後、ヨーロッパから登山というスポーツが伝わってきても、なかなか広まらなかったのも、この心理的な呪縛が残っていたからだ。

　日本人の登山家第1号は、小島烏水という人

stall. Since they're all in it together, they don't care if they happen to see each other.

However, people outside a restroom have no interest in what goes on inside. That's why Europeans and Americans dislike the design of Japanese restrooms so much.

This may be a culture gap, as many Japanese probably are unable to understand this Western attitude.

Q: Why was Japan so late to start the sport of mountain climbing?

A: Many Japanese mountain climbers now want to conquer Mount Everest. But even though Japan has many mountains, it wasn't until the early twentieth century that the sport appeared in Japan.

In Europe, mountain climbing was popular as long ago as the eighteenth century. Japan was a late-comer partly, of course, due to Japan's self-imposed isolation. But a more important reason was the attitude of the people toward mountains.

In Japan, mountains were considered sacred places imbued with a religious aura. They were where Buddhist ascetics practiced their rigorous self-discipline. Among common people, mountains inspired both awe and fear. They were so forbidding that no one ever considered climbing them. Even after people learned about mountain climbing from Europeans following the Meiji Restoration of 1868, the sport gained little popularity at first. People had not broken free of the mountains' psychological grip.

The first Japanese mountain climber was a man named

物。明治35年（1902年）、槍ヶ岳の初登頂に成功している。日本アルプスを縦断してみせたイギリスのウォルター・ウェストンが、日本に近代登山を紹介してから10年後のことだった。

小島烏水は、その後「山岳会」を設立し、日本での登山普及につとめた。山岳会は、明治42年（1909年）に「日本山岳会」へと発展し、以後、日本人のあいだにも登山熱が急速に広まっていった。

Q: 日本人は、なぜ英語が下手なのか？

A: ————— ある日本人が、「外国で、英語に困ったことがない」と豪語したあと、「その代わり、相手が困ってる」と笑っていた。こんな人は、有名ブランド店で、「コストダウン。あかんか、ネエちゃん」と叫んでいるタイプ。これでは、相手の店員が困るだろうが、日本人のなかには、笑えない人が多いはずである。

日本人の英語下手は、発音が悪いせいでもあるのだが、その元凶は、第一に中学、高校の英語教育にあるといえる。

最近多少は改善されているようであるが、中学、高校の英語の授業は、やはり文法と読みが中心。英語の発音の仕方を習うより、文章がいかに正確に読めるかが優先されがちである。そのため、生徒も、単語と文法を覚えることに精力を傾ける。

Kojima Usui. In 1902, he made the first ascent of Yarigatake in the northern Japan Alps. That success came a decade after Walter Weston of Britain had introduced modern mountain climbing to Japan by hiking across the Japan Alps.

Kojima Usui later founded the Alpine Club and worked to promote mountain climbing in his country. In 1909, the organization was renamed the Japan Alpine Club. Enthusiasm for mountain climbing grew quickly thereafter.

Q: Why are the Japanese so inept at English?

A: A Japanese person once bragged, "I never have problems with English when I go abroad." Laughing, he continued, "I only make problems for the people I talk to."

That's the kind of Japanese person who, when shopping in a famous store overseas, will shout at the clerks in a mixture of ersatz English and rough Japanese vernacular. Those clerks do have problems with such customers. For many Japanese, though, the man's joke cuts a bit too close to the bone for laughter.

Part of the reason for the poor English ability of the Japanese is their bad pronunciation. But the real source of their linguistic awkwardness is English-language education in Japanese junior high and high schools.

Although some improvements have been made recently, English classes in secondary schools still concentrate only on grammar and reading. Rather than learning how to pronounce English, students spend more time learning to read English texts correctly. They put all of their efforts into remembering vocabulary and grammar.

英語の発音が下手なのは、ちゃんと教えてもらっていないせいだが、その代わり、旅先でみる掲示や注意書き、新聞などを読むことはできる。会話は下手でも、読む力は十分にあるタイプが多いのである。

　考えてみると、少し前まで日本では、外国人と話すより、英字新聞や洋書を読む機会のほうが多かった。つまり、英語教育も、必要に合わせて読解力中心だったのである。

　そんな時代に育った日本人に、いきなり英語をうまく話せといっても無理な話。カタカナ英語に慣れきった口からは、いわゆる "ジャパニーズ・イングリッシュ" しか出てこないのが当然なのである。

Q: なぜ、日本では下水道の普及が遅れたのか？

A: ――――水洗トイレに慣れた日本の子供には、地方のくみ取り便所では、用を足せないことがあるという。怖くて、出るものも、出なくなってしまうのである。

　都会の人は、こんなエピソードを笑うだろうが、比較的大きな地方都市でも、まだ下水道が完備していないところは多い。ヨーロッパの先進国に比べて、日本は、下水道の普及が大幅に遅れているのである。日本が、ヨーロッパ諸国に比べて遅れているのは、中世のころから、排泄物の扱いが大きく違っていたからである。

　中世のヨーロッパでは、排泄物は、窓から道路へ捨てるのが一般的だった。路上には、糞尿

Japanese pronounce English poorly because they are never really taught proper pronunciation. When traveling overseas, though, they can generally read English signs, warnings, and newspapers. Many have good reading skills even if they can't hold a conversation.

Until recently, the Japanese had more chances to read English newspapers or foreign books than talk with foreigners. This explains why English-language education focused on reading skills.

Japanese people brought up in that era should not be expected to suddenly be able to speak English well. It's no surprise that only ersatz English emerges from mouths that have never spoken any English.

Q: Why were sewerage systems developed so slowly in Japan?

A: Japanese children who are used to flush toilets are often unable to use commodes that sit above septic tanks. They need to go, but they're so afraid that they can't.

City people laugh at such stories, but many fairly large cities and towns in Japan still do not have complete sewerage systems. Compared with developed countries in Europe, Japan still fags behind in the development of sewers. The reason for this tardiness is the fact that ever since the Middle Ages human wastes have been handled very differently in Europe and Japan.

In medieval Europe, people used to throw their night soil out of the window and onto the road. The streets

や残飯が散乱するほど汚かった。そのため、大都市に人口が集中すると、排泄物と悪臭で衛生状態は最悪。19世紀、コレラが大流行して数万人が死んだのをきっかけに、近代的な下水道の整備がすすめられたのである。

ところが、日本では、昔から、排泄物は農家が肥料としてつかってきた。便所もくみ取り式で、河川を汚す心配もなかった。戦後、さすがに大都市では下水道がかなり整備されたが、地方では、ほとんど十数年前まで排泄物は農家の肥料につかわれてきたのである。

ところが、化学肥料が普及して、排泄物が見捨てられた。さらに、高度経済成長期に、生活排水が汚れ、下水道整備が、緊急課題となった。

しかし、すでに道路が整備されていた地域で、下水道工事は、いちいち道路を掘り返す必要があった。お金と時間がかかるため、下水道工事は、なかなかすすんでいないのである。全国の下水道の普及率は、1993年で47パーセント。やっと、全国の半分の整備が終わったところである。

Q: 日本の米は、なぜ他国より高いのか？

A: ————「ライス大盛りでお願いします」という値段が、「100円増」。そんな食生活を送っている人に、日本の米は高いといっても、実感はないかもしれない。

would be awash in feces, urine, and kitchen scraps. As the population of large cities increased, the wastes and smells posed a horrible problem for sanitation. After a nineteenth-century cholera epidemic left tens of thousands of people dead, the construction of modern sewers began.

Since ancient times in Japan, though, night soil has been used by farmers as fertilizer. The toilets were designed so that the waste could be scooped up and used, so there was no worry about polluting rivers either. After World War II, sewerage systems were built in larger cities, but human waste continued to be used as fertilizer in rural areas until just a decade or two ago.

As chemical fertilizers became commonplace, collecting night soil was forgotten. During Japan's period of rapid economic growth in the 1960s, pollution from households toilets became so bad that the construction of sewers was an urgent necessity.

By that time, though, many areas already had paved streets, and to put in sewers meant that the streets had to be dug up. Sewerage construction is thus both expensive and time-consuming, so it has been proceeding slowly. By 1993, 47 percent of Japan, or half the country, had sewers.

Q: Why is Japanese rice more expensive than rice in other countries?

A: If you ask for extra rice at a Japanese restaurant, the price might be only 100 yen more. For people used to such prices, Japanese rice may not seem very expensive.

ところが、米屋やスーパーで、お米を買うようになると、その高さを実感する。じっさい、日本の米の値段は、アメリカの3倍、タイの7〜8倍もする。物価の違いといえばそれまでだが、日本の米が高いのには、それなりの理由がある。

　たとえば、タイの米が安いのは、米が重要な輸出品だからである。中近東やアジア諸国に米を売りこむためには、国際競争力を考えて、つねに米の値段を安くしておく必要がある。いわば、輸出戦略上、タイ国内に流通する米の値段も安く抑えられているのである。

　また、アメリカの米が安いのは、大規模経営によるところが大きい。1軒の農家が、日本の200倍ぐらいの田に、飛行機でタネをまき、大型コンバインで収穫する。生産コストが低いために、値段も安くなる。

　ところが、日本は、国際競争力も関係なければ、大規模経営のメリットもない。それどころか、小さな田を耕すのに、農機具をローンで購入するなど、やたらと経費をかけて、米をつくる。だから日本の米は高いのである。

Q: 日本の基礎研究は、なぜ立ち遅れているのか？

A: ────── 経済は一流でも、政治は三流といわれるニッポン。「では、学術面は？」というと、二流から二流半というのが、一般的な見方。

　たとえば、ノーベル賞受賞者の数をみると、200人を超えるアメリカには遠く及ばないにし

If you buy rice at a rice shop or supermarket, though, you'll understand how expensive it is. In fact, Japanese rice costs three times more than American rice and seven to eight times more than Thai rice. That's due partly to different overall price levels, but there are also other reasons for Japan's high rice prices.

Thai rice is cheap because it's an important export for that country. In order to remain competitive in Middle East or Asian markets, Thai merchants have to keep their prices low. As part of its export strategy, Thailand must keep the price of domestic rice prices low as well.

In the United States, it's large-scale agribusiness that keeps rice cheap. A single farm might have fields that are two hundred times the size of a Japanese farm. Farm workers use airplanes to plant the seed and huge combines to harvest the rice. Production costs are low, and so are rice prices.

In Japan, though, there's no need to worry about international competitiveness, and farmers cannot benefit from economies of scale. Instead, they borrow money to buy equipment to farm their tiny plots, thus raising their costs even more. That's why Japanese rice is so expensive.

Q: Why does Japan lag so far behind in basic research?

A: Japan is said to have a first-rate economy and third-rate politics. If you wonder about Japanese scholarship, most people would say it's second-rate or even second-and-a-half rate.

Look at the number of its Nobel Prize recipients. With seven Nobel laureates, Japan ranks fourteenth, far behind

ても、過去に7人で14位。7人のなかには、佐藤栄作元首相の平和賞などもふくまれるが、物理や化学といった分野のノーベル賞は、もっぱら、偉大な基礎研究に与えられる賞。その基礎研究で、日本は、ほかの先進国に比べてかなり弱いのである。

たしかに、産業と結びついた企業の研究は、日本も高いレベルにある。それに対して、大学の基礎研究が弱いのは、若手の研究者が、思い切って好きな研究に打ちこめないことに理由があるという。

たとえば日本の大学でやっているのは、ほとんどが他国の後追い研究。「日本に留学した意味がない」と、外国人留学生も怒っているが、すでに発表された欧米の科学者の論文を確認する研究ばかりしているから、進歩がない。

だからといって、教授の方針に刃向かえば、研究室にいられなくなる。教授が権威主義的で、自分の興味にそった研究をしたくても、させてもらえないからである。助教授、教授と、大学で出世したければ、担当教授の興味に従って、後追い研究をするほかないのである。

もっとも、最近は、教授の質がどうでも、だまって教授に従うタイプの学生が増えているという。これも、小学生のときからの偏差値教育の弊害なのだろうか。

the United States, which has over two hundred winners. And Japan's seven winners include former Prime Minister Satō Eisaku, who received the Nobel Peace Prize. The Nobel Prize in fields like physics and chemistry is given mainly for basic research, and that's where Japan lags far behind other industrialized countries.

It's true that the level of industrial research by Japanese companies is quite high. The reason for the country's weakness at basic university research is that young researchers are unable to work on the subjects they're interested in.

Almost all the research done at Japanese universities is aimed at catching up with other countries. Foreign students have complained that it's a waste of time to study in Japan. Since all Japanese researchers do is try to confirm the results announced by scientists in Europe and America, no progress is made.

If a young Japanese researcher should go against the policy of his advising professor, he'll be unable to stay in that professor's research group. Professorial authority prevents students from following their own research interests. If a student wants to rise through the university ranks to assistant professor and then to professor, he has no choice but to do the catch-up research his adviser cares about.

Recently it's been said that, regardless of the caliber of the professors, more and more students just silently do their advisers' bidding. Perhaps they are unable to shake off the damage caused by the competitive, exam-based learning in which they have been immersed since elementary school.

Q: 日本人は、なぜ自己主張が下手なのか？

A: ────── 日本人がアメリカで暮らすと、「どうして、そんなに謙虚なんだ」「おとなしいんだ」といわれる。ところが、同じ人が日本に帰ってくると、「どうして、おまえは、そんなに自己主張が強いんだ」といわれてしまう。

というくらい、日米の対人関係のスタンダードには、ギャップがある。アメリカ人にとって、積極的に自己主張するのは当然のことだが、日本人は自己主張を抑え、組織・集団の和を大事にしていくことを優先する。自分を殺すことに、かぎりなく美徳を感じる国民ともいえる。

こういう性格は、すでに子供の性格調査ではっきり表れる。アメリカの幼児には、能動的な性格が顕著で、日本の幼児は受動的な性格があらわれる。

専門家によると、これは乳児・幼児期の育て方の違いによるところが大きいという。日本の場合、母親が子供といっしょに過ごす時間が長く、相当大きくなるまで添い寝をしたり、いっしょに入浴する。

そういう生活のなかでは、子供たちは、母親に対して、とくに自己主張をする必要がない。自己主張しなくても、大事にしてもらえるわけだ。

一方、アメリカでは、赤ん坊のときから、個室に寝かせられるなど、母親と接触する時間は短い。そこで、泣くなどの表現で母親の注意を喚起することが、たえず必要になる。それが、自己主張の芽生えになるという。

Q: Why are the Japanese so poor at asserting themselves?

A: If a Japanese person lives in the United States, he or she is likely to be called "quiet" or "modest." When he or she returns to Japan, though, people will ask, "Why are you so assertive?"

This shows the huge gap between standards for interpersonal relations in the U.S. and Japan. Americans take strong self-assertiveness for granted, while Japanese try to be unassertive and to give priority to harmony with the organization or group. In Japan, people feel that suppressing the self is the ultimate virtue.

These differences appear clearly even in surveys of children's personalities. American babies have distinctly active personalities, while young Japanese children are passive.

According to experts, a large role is played by the difference in child-rearing practices during infancy and early childhood. In Japan, mothers spend much time with their children and continue to sleep and bathe with them until the children are quite big. Living like that, the children don't need to assert themselves to their mothers, because they will still be taken care of.

In America, though, babies sleep in separate rooms and spend less time with their mothers. They constantly have to cry or express themselves in other ways to draw their mothers' attention. This marks the beginning of their self-assertiveness.

それぞれに、三つ子の魂百まで。その差を埋めるのはなかなかむずかしそうだ。

Q: 日本の在来種は、なぜ帰化動物より弱いのか?

A: ──────── 小川でみかけるザリガニのほとんどは、アメリカザリガニである。もともと、日本にはいなかった種類だが、1930年、アメリカからもちこまれると、たちまち大繁殖。日本の小川に、はびこるようになった。

このアメリカザリガニのように、外国から日本にやってきて棲み着いた動物を「帰化動物」と呼ぶが、この帰化動物の生命力が、やたら強い。

環境が変わっても、適応力が強いということもある。しかし、それ以上に、古い時代から、島国で生きてきた在来種が、原始的で弱い種が多いことが原因とされている。日本の在来種が、帰化動物にやられてしまうのである。

たとえば、アメリカザリガニがもちこまれた理由は、ウシガエルのエサとしてだった。神奈川県大船町へ200匹が送られ、無事に着いたのは、わずか20匹。このなかの数匹が逃げだし、その30年後には、本州、九州、四国の大部分に生息していった。ものすごい適応力を発揮しながら、日本産のザリガニを追っ払って西日本を中心に勢力を広げたのである。

また、1930年ごろにもちこまれたチョウセンイタチも、在来のニホンイタチを押し退けるように西日本ではびこった。チョウセンイタチが、

As the Japanese proverb says, "The spirit of the three-year-old stays the same at age one hundred," so it is not easy to narrow the gap between different personality types.

Q: Why are Japan's indigenous animals so much weaker than "naturalized" species?

A: Almost all crayfish seen in Japanese streams are American crayfish. They did not live in Japan originally, but after they were brought from America in 1930 they spread quickly. They now run rampant in streams in Japan.

Species like the American crayfish that were brought from other countries and have taken residence in Japan are called "naturalized" animals, and they have enormous vitality.

One reason for their success is that they adapt easily to new environments. A more important reason is that the native species that have lived on the Japanese islands for millennia are often weaker and more primitive. The natives get clobbered by the interlopers.

The American crayfish were introduced to Japan as food for bullfrogs. Two hundred of the animals were brought to Ōfuna-machi in Kanagawa Prefecture, but only about twenty managed to survive. A few of those escaped. Three decades later, the American crustaceans had taken up residence throughout most of Honshu, Kyushu, and Shikoku. As they adapted superbly and spread throughout western Japan, they drove out the native crayfish.

Also introduced around 1930 was the Korean weasel. It overpowered the native Japanese weasel and flourished in Western Japan. The Korean weasel is a stronger, more

ニホンイタチより進化した強い種であったため、勢力争いにも簡単に勝っていったのである。

　現在もなお、北海道のミンク、岐阜のアライグマ、鎌倉のタイワンリス、下北（青森県北東部）のタイワンザルなどの帰化動物が、在来種を制圧しつつある。

Q: なぜ、ニホンオオカミは絶滅したのか？

A: ──────女の子をアパートまで送って、「トイレ貸してくれる？」と部屋にあがる "送りオオカミ" は、ますます増えているようだが、本物のニホンオオカミは、ずいぶん昔に絶滅している。

　江戸時代までは、夜になると、人家のまばらな街道筋に出没。道端に放置された馬や牛の死骸をエサにしながら、ときには人を襲うこともあって、恐れられていた。

　当時、それほど多くのニホンオオカミがいたのに、絶滅してしまったのは、人間の銃と病気のせいである。すでに、江戸時代には、銃の性能がよくなって、狩猟がさかんになった。そこで、猟師は、人間を襲うニホンオオカミを標的にして、どんどん撃ち殺した。そのため、急速に数が減っていった。

　とどめとなったのは、伝染病の流行。明治になってから、飼い犬から感染したと思われる伝染病が、オオカミ社会に蔓延。群れをつくって行動していたニホンオオカミは、ほとんど絶滅してしまったのである。

highly evolved species, so it easily won the struggle for dominance.

Other naturalized animals that are now overpowering native species include the mink in Hokkaido, the raccoon in Gifu, the Taiwan squirrel in Kamakura, and the Taiwan monkey in Shimokita, northeast Aomori Prefecture.

Q: Why did the Japanese wolf become extinct?

A: Some wolves are growing in number, like the lascivious "wolves" who try to take advantage of young women by seeing them home to their apartments and then asking to use the bathroom. The genuine Japanese wolf, though, became extinct long ago.

Up through the Edo period, these wolves would appear on roads in lightly populated areas and devour the remnants of horses and cattle abandoned along the roadside. The wolves were feared, as they would sometimes attack people as well.

Although there were many Japanese wolves then, they disappeared for two reasons: guns and disease. By the Edo period, guns became more efficient in Japan and hunting became popular. Because wolves attacked people, they became the target of hunters, who slaughtered them by the hundreds. The animals quickly decreased in number.

The final blow was an epidemic of infectious disease. In the Meiji period, the illness probably caught from domesticated dogs spread through the wolf communities. As the Japanese wolves always moved in packs, they were soon wiped out.

本作品は1996年9月、河出書房新社で刊行された『「なぜ?」がわかる博学BOOK② ニッポンの謎篇』を改訂し、英訳をつけました。

英語で話す「雑学ニッポン」Q&A
Japan Trivia

1998年11月13日　第 1 刷発行
2008年 1 月31日　第11刷発行

著　者　　素朴な疑問探究会

発行者　　富田 充

発行所　　講談社インターナショナル株式会社
　　　　　〒112-8652　東京都文京区音羽 1-17-14
　　　　　電話　03-3944-6493（編集部）
　　　　　　　　03-3944-6492（営業部・業務部）
　　　　　ホームページ　www.kodansha-intl.com

印刷・製本所　大日本印刷株式会社

© 素朴な疑問探究会 1998
Printed in Japan
ISBN 978-4-7700-2361-2